EYEWITNESS
TO HISTORY

EYEWITNESS
TO HISTORY

RODNEY CASTLEDEN

canary
press

This paperback edition published by Canary Press in 2011

© Canary Press 2011

This book was previously published in hardback as *Witness to History*
© Omnipress Limited 2008

A CIP catalogue record for this book is available from the
British Library.

ISBN: 978-1-907795-61-9

Cover and internal design: Anthony Prudente on behalf of
Omnipress Limited.

Printed and bound in Great Britain

Canary Press is an imprint of Omnipress Limited,
Chantry House, 22 Upperton Road,
Eastbourne, East Sussex BN21 1BF

For Susan and Frank Drader

CONTENTS

CONTENTS

INTRODUCTION

History is the version of the past that we are most familiar with, the version which has been thought about most, mulled over most, the events fully analysed and assessed. History is a considered and self-conscious account of events, usually assembled long after they have happened – and it is an account of events that has enormous value to us. We like to think of history as objectively true, but as we shall see that is not always the case.

Though we think of it as being a commentary on the present, journalism is really another take on the past, a close-up and speeded-up version of the past. It is presented immediately after the events have happened, and it often carries much of their immediacy. A good, well-written piece of journalism can make it seem as if we are actually present at the events described, as if we ourselves are witnesses. Because of the speed with which journalists have to work, close up to their editors' deadlines, their stories may contain mistakes, and they are often incomplete. The end result is that what we read in newspapers and magazines has a very different texture from history.

Then there is the eye-witness account, a version of the past that is more immediate still. Some of the eye-witness accounts, even those written by ordinary people, have an extraordinary eloquence; this seems to tell us that people can be lifted up by the experience of witnessing some remarkable or momentous happening. One such account is the description of Thomas Becket's assassination by an ordinary monk who just happened to be visiting Canterbury that day in 1170, and got caught up in the epic event of a martyrdom that fired the imagination of medieval Europe for the next three centuries. His name was Edward Grim, and he led a life of total obscurity – apart from this one shining moment when he stood side by side with a saint as he was murdered. And his account verges on the visionary. Another account that is surprisingly eloquent is Che Guevara's account of the Cuban Revolution. Che Guevara was very much the man of action – and yet he wrote extremely well.

The great attraction of the account of an eye-witness is that, however long afterwards we may be reading it, it gives us the feeling of what it would have been like to be there, caught up in the moment of some historic event. That gives it a special interest. Eye-witness accounts are sometimes seen as more truthful than the historians' accounts, because historians often have a political perspective, an agenda, an 'angle' on the past. For instance, we have to be sceptical of Sir Thomas More's account of the reign of Richard III because he was an apologist for the Tudor monarchs; More was bound to denigrate Richard III in order to justify the seizure of the English throne from Richard by Henry VII, who was the father of his patron, Henry VIII.

But even the accounts of eye-witnesses have to be treated with caution. We are all sometimes mistaken in what we think we have seen or heard, especially if we are caught off-guard by sudden events. Because of our personalities, interests and shortcomings, we notice some things and not others. Because of our religious persuasion, social and economic background or political affiliation, we may choose to emphasize some aspects of an event rather than others – not out of a desire to mislead but simply because some things interest us much more than others. Because of our own personal involvement, we may consciously or unconsciously slant the story. This slanting becomes very apparent when there are several eye-witness accounts of an event. In a simple everyday event like a minor road accident, there is the account of the injured party (the man whose car is shunted), the account of the perpetrator of the accident (the man who carelessly drives into the back of the other man's vehicle) and the account of the bystander, who is watching (or maybe not really watching) from the pavement. The three accounts will be quite different from one another, and in entirely predictable ways.

We have to allow for bias, which may be the result of social, political, racial or religious background. But sometimes when we assume an account is distorted by bias we may find we are wrong. A classic example of this is Alexander Werth's horrific account of the Maidanek death camp. That was assumed by the BBC to be biased because Werth, though a naturalized Briton, had been born in Russia. It was also assumed to be too extreme – the BBC thought that the Nazi prison camps could not possibly have been as bad as that - but Werth's account turned out to be all too true.

By contrast, in some other situations, what at first appears to be a bland and objective account may turn out to have been tailored in some way to reflect and emphasize the perceptions and interests of the witness. Queen Victoria's account of her accession tells us of her sense of the dignity of the historic moment and of her new-found independence of mind; Charles Greville's account of the young queen's coronation tells us, by contrast, of a distinct lack of dignity in that occasion as he saw it, because of the lack of rehearsal. Julius Caesar's account of what he did as a military commander inevitably contains a lot of self-justification and self-congratulation; the whole point of his reminiscence is to impress Roman readers with his brilliance as a military commander – it is his CV, his platform for high political office in Rome. No doubt a very different account would have been given by his victims, the late iron age tribes of France and Britain, but they were for the most part non-literate. Writing things down was not part of their culture, so we do not have their accounts to balance Caesar's.

Some accounts appear straightforward, when they are far from straightforward. Howard Carter's account of his own opening of the tomb of Tutankhamun gives no hint, no clue, of the fairly high level of deception in which Carter was engaging. His account reads as if it is true, but it isn't.

Sometimes the bias makes for a more interesting eye-witness account in that the witness has succeeded in overcoming it. Priscus' impression of Attila the Hun is a classic example of a strongly biased observer arriving on a scene and then overcoming his bias. Like many another citizen of the Roman Empire, Priscus was predisposed to see Attila as a savage. In reality he was a civilized, modest and moderate man with elaborate formal table manners, very like a Roman emperor, in fact.

It is accounts like this, where the principles, beliefs and prejudices of the onlooker are really put to the test and prejudices overcome, that we should value – treasure, even. They are the unassailably truthful accounts, we can be sure.

Another reason for valuing first-hand accounts is the contemporary eye for particular detail.

Exactly how humane was the execution of Mary Queen of Scots? Where exactly did the sound of the gunfire come from – to the ears of those actually standing in Dealey Plaza that day in Dallas in 1963?

There were many 'Joe Public' or 'man in the street' witnesses to the Kennedy assassination, all literate too, and their testimonies were all duly recorded by the Warren Commission. Ultimately it is those testimonies, collectively, with all their intriguing and sometimes mystifying inconsistencies and contradictions, which must become the raw material of history. History cannot be written without the accounts of witnesses. After the Second World War, the surviving German leaders were put on trial. The distinguished journalist Walter Cronkite was chief correspondent of United Press in the mid-1940s, and he observed, 'Those of us who witnessed the Nuremberg Trials, as well as those who organized and participated in them, were highly conscious of the fact that history was being made.'

Many of the witnesses in this book are bystanders or non-players in the events of history. Priscus, Edward Grim, Dr Beatty, Marie-Louise Osmont, Vincent Sheean and Jean Hill fall into this group. They were ordinary people caught up in great events. Their accounts have a special resonance because they stand in for us, for the ordinary people who just happen, sometimes, to be in the right place at the right moment, to see some historic event unfold. There are also witnesses who are far from being bystanders; they are major players, sometimes central players, in the events they are describing, which makes them fascinating from a different point of view. Into this group fall Plato, Columbus, Guy Fawkes, Orville Wright, Captain Scott and Howard Carter. These people are far more than witnesses - they are themselves the makers of history.

In the remote past very few of the witnesses to historic events were literate and, with some high-profile exceptions like Julius Caesar, even the literate witnesses did not write their reminiscences.

The business of writing down was left to scribes, clerks, monks. The ancient accounts were often proxy accounts, memoirs written down by others. The account of the death of Socrates was written down by Plato following detailed interviews with those who witnessed it. There is a particular poignancy about this account, because Plato was conscious that as a friend of Socrates he should have been there himself. He should have been an eye-witness, but when the moment came he did not have the courage.

In all of the accounts that follow the original text has been respected; that is to say that the text has been quoted word for word, and not paraphrased. The only editorial interventions are that spellings have been modernized, because antique spellings usually get in the way of the meaning, and in some places the punctuation has been modernized to improve the readability and clarify the meaning. Many of the accounts have been edited down somewhat to bring them to a manageable length, but this has been done with care, so as to avoid changing either the emphasis or the style of the original.

I ought to mention here that in the account of the Ku Klux Klan, the word 'nigger' is used. It is a word that would often cause offence when used in a modern context, but it must be remembered that this is the word that was actually used by Ben Johnson, himself a black ex-slave, to describe his own kind in the year 1868. Time and ideas of political correctness change; a century later, and the word would usually be taken as a term of racist abuse, and a very objectionable one at that. It is very important to read each account in this book as a reflection of the particular time and culture that produced it.

THE DEATH OF SOCRATES

Of all the men of his time whom I have known, he was the wisest, the justest, the best.

WITNESSED BY
PLATO

The Greek philosopher Socrates had the reputation of being the wisest man of his age, yet in 400 BC the Athenians put him on trial charged with not worshipping the gods of Athens and for corrupting the young. He was tried before a court of over 500 citizen-judges, found guilty by a narrow majority and condemned to death by poison. It was regarded in the ancient world as a scandalous miscarriage of justice. Socrates himself was indifferent to the sentence. He was allowed to spend his last day in lengthy philosophical conversations with his friends and pupils, before drinking hemlock and dying in their presence.

THE WITNESS

Plato (about 428–348 BC) was one of the most influential philosophers of ancient Greece. Practically everything we know about the philosopher Socrates (469-399 BC) comes from the writings of Plato. Plato was the teacher of

Aristotle and one of Socrates' devoted friends and pupils. As such he should have been present at Socrates' enforced suicide, but he conspicuously was not. Probably he was frightened of being associated with the condemned man. In his dialogue *Phaedo*, Plato imagined himself there, vividly reconstructing the scene as a docu-drama from the eye-witness reports of his friends. The knowledge that he *should* have been a witness probably haunted him for the rest of his life.

Athens in 400 BC

Athenian society in 400 BC was made up of four main bands. The upper class, the metics (or middle class), the lower class – made up of freemen of foreign birth and former slaves, and slaves. To qualify as a member of the Athenian upper class one would have to be a citizen that did not require employment. These aristocrats were free from economic tasks of any kind. These members of 'the leisure class' had slaves to take care of any material concerns, which freed up much time for participation in politics, war, literature and philosophy. Every other part of Athenian society was employed in one way or another, even Socrates himself made his living initially as a stonemason. This explains why Socrates' followers were all aristocrats, they were the only people who had enough spare time to learn from him. The entire Athenian aristocracy was tiny; it consisted of no more than 300 families. The teachings of Socrates inspired and informed the younger generation of upper class Athenians and, in turn, Greek culture heavily influenced the Romans – who carried these ideas to wider Europe.

THE WITNESS SETS THE SCENE

He turned to us, and added with a smile: 'I cannot make Crito believe that I am the same

Socrates who has been talking and conducting the argument; he fancies that I am the other Socrates whom he will soon see, a dead body - and he asks, How shall he bury me? I have tried to explain that when I have drunk the poison I shall leave you and go to the joys of the blessed – but I can see these words of comfort have had no effect upon Crito. I would not have him sorrow at my hard lot. Be of good cheer, my dear Crito, and say that you are burying my body only, and do with that whatever is usual, and what you think best.'

He arose and went to bathe; Crito followed him and told us to wait. So we remained behind, talking and thinking of the greatness of our sorrow; he was like a father of whom we were being bereaved, and we were about to pass the rest of our lives as orphans. When he had taken the bath his children were brought to him (he had two young sons and an elder one); and the women of his family also came; then he dismissed them and returned to us.

Character Profiles

Plato

Plato was the youngest son of Ariston and Perictione, who both came from wealthy and famous Athenian families. When he was still very young, his father died and his mother remarried, so he grew up mostly in the house of his stepfather, Pyrilampes. Plato was not his birth name, but rather a nickname – meaning broad – given to him because of his large build. As a young man Plato studied poetry and music as well as metaphysics and epistemology, but it was in Socrates that Plato met his definitive teacher – a man whom he evidently saw as a father figure. Perhaps this devotion explains why he could not find the courage to be present at the execution of Socrates.

Socrates

Socrates has become widely perceived as the father of Western Philosophy. His charisma and commitment to truth and justice meant he was able to inspire near-fanatical devotion in his students. His pupils were often rich young aristocrats whose prestigious parents disapproved of their teacher's methods and views. Socrates routinely questioned his pupils' often unwavering faith in the common perceptions of the day – and this is the main reason why he was so unpopular with the Athenian establishment. Despite his unpopularity, his execution was dignified compared with the treatment given to most criminals of the time, who would have been unceremoniously thrown from the Acropolis into a pit full of spikes. His death was certainly that of a nobleman.

....

Crito

Crito was a wealthy and very loyal friend of Socrates who visited him in prison and proposed the idea of paying off the informers and the prison guards in order to allow Socrates to escape from jail and thus avoid the death sentence awaiting him. Crito made it plain that he was willing to suffer punishment in order to save the life of his friend and teacher. Socrates argued that one injustice cannot be resolved with another, no matter what motivates it. According to Plato's version of events, Socrates had accepted that this was his fate and only hoped his followers could also accept it.

THE WITNESS'S ACCOUNT

Now the hour of sunset was near. When he came out, he sat down with us again, but not much was said. Soon the jailer entered and stood by him, saying: 'To you, Socrates, whom I know to be the noblest and gentlest and best of all who ever came to this place, I will not impute the angry feelings of other men, who rage and swear at me, when, in obedience to the authorities, I bid them drink the poison - indeed, I am sure that you will not be angry with me; for others, as you are aware, and not I, are to blame. So fare you well, and try to bear lightly what must needs be; you know my errand.' Then he burst into tears and went out.

Socrates turned to us and said, 'How charming the man is: since I have been in prison he has always been coming to see me, and was as good to me as could be. Now see how generously he sorrows on my account. We must do as he says, Crito. Let the cup be brought, if the poison is prepared; if not, let the attendant prepare some.'

Crito said, 'But the sun is still upon the hilltops, and I know that many a one has taken the draught late, and after the announcement has been made to him he has eaten and drunk, and enjoyed the society of his beloved. Do not hurry. There is time enough.'

....

"When the poison reaches the heart, that will be the end."

....

Socrates said, 'Yes, Crito, and they are right, because they think that they will gain by the delay. But I do not think that I should gain anything by drinking the poison a little later. I should only be ridiculous in my own eyes for sparing a life which is already forfeit. Please do as I say, and do not refuse me.'

Crito made a sign to the servant who was standing by; and he went out, and after some time returned with the jailer carrying the cup of poison. Socrates said: 'You, my good friend, are experienced in these matters. Give me directions how I am to proceed.'

The man answered, 'You have only to walk about until your legs are heavy. Then lie down, and the poison will act.'

He handed the cup to Socrates, who gently looked the man straight in the eye, as his manner was, and took the cup. He said: 'What do you say about making a libation out of this cup? May I do that?'

The man answered. 'Socrates, we only prepare just as much as we deem necessary.'

'I understand,' he said, 'but I must ask the gods to prosper my journey to the other world. So be it according to my prayer.'

Then he raised the cup to his lips, and quite

cheerfully drank the poison. Until then, most of us had been able to control our sorrow. But now we saw him drinking, we could not control ourselves. In spite of myself my tears flowed fast; I covered my face and wept, not for him, but for my own loss. Crito found himself unable to restrain his tears; I followed. Then Apollodorus, who had been weeping all the time, broke out in a loud and passionate cry.

Socrates alone kept calm. 'What is this strange outcry?' he said. 'I sent the women away so that they would not misbehave in this way. A man should die in peace. Be quiet, and have patience.'

We stifled our tears. He walked about until his legs began to fail, then lay on his back, according to the directions. The man who had given him the poison now and then looked at his feet and legs. After a while he pressed his foot and asked him if he could feel it, and he said, 'No'. Then his leg, and so on further and further up and showed us that he was cold and stiff. And he felt them himself, and said,

'When the poison reaches the heart, that will be the end.'

He was beginning to grow cold about the groin, when he uncovered his face, for he had covered himself up. Then he said - they were his last words – 'Crito, I owe a cock to Asclepius. Will you remember to pay the debt?'

'The debt shall be paid,' said Crito. 'Is there anything else?' There was no answer; in a minute or two there was a movement. The attendants uncovered him. His eyes were fixed, and Crito closed his eyes and mouth.

Such was the end of our friend. Of all the men of his time whom I have known, he was the wisest, the justest, the best.

THE ASSASSINATION OF JULIUS CAESAR

All quickly unsheathed their daggers and rushed at him

WITNESSED BY
NICOLAUS OF DAMASCUS

By 45 BC, Julius Caesar (102-44 BC) had a string of impressive military conquests behind him. He had become the most powerful figure in the Roman world. Some Romans were alarmed at the development of a personal dictatorship. Honours that Julius Caesar said he did not want were heaped upon him. When his friend Mark Antony offered him the diadem of kingship, a conspiracy to murder Caesar was hatched. The chief conspirators were Gaius Cassius Longinus and Marcus Junius Brutus, both of whom had been pardoned by Caesar. They persuaded others to join them in assassinating him.

THE WITNESS

Nicolaus of Damascus was a Syrian philosopher and historian, born in Damascus. He was a close friend of King Herod the Great. Nicolaus's chief work was a monumental *Universal History*, a history in 144 volumes. Unfortunately only a few fragments of this have survived. One surviving work is his biography of Augustus, which includes the account of Julius Caesar's assassination. Shortly after the assassination Nicolaus arrived in Rome, where he had the opportunity to interview several eye-witnesses. His account was written a few years after the event and is believed to be reliable. As an outsider, he was an objective and impartial observer. He saw what happened as a crude and mismanaged bid for power. He was familiar with the Greek concept of liberty as a cause, and was not taken in by the assassins' claim to be the liberators of Rome.

Superstition and Roman society

The Romans were very superstitious. They lived in a world full of unexplained phenomena, which they chose to interpret in supernatural rather than scientific terms. The Roman obsession with interpreting natural events as signs from the supernatural world was inherited from the Etruscans; the reading of omens to predict the future was raised to the status of a science.

Romans of all kinds believed that the future could be read using the entrails of sacrificial animals, the liver and the heart being of particular importance in the process. In the days before his murder, Caesar is said to have killed a wild animal and opened it up, only to discover, to his horror, that it had no heart. There were other bad omens around at the time of Caesar's assassination, strange, fiery creatures were apparently seen fighting around the forum, and various soothsayers predicted that the 'Ides of March' would bring with it dramatic change.

THE WITNESS SETS THE SCENE

The conspirators never met openly, but they assembled a few at a time in each others' homes. There were many discussions and proposals, as might be expected, while they investigated how and where to execute their design. Some suggested that they should make the attempt as he [Julius Caesar] was going along the Sacred Way, which was one of his favourite walks. Another idea was for it to be done at the elections during which he had to cross a bridge to appoint the magistrates in the Field of Mars; they should draw lots for some to push him off the bridge and others to run up and kill him. A third plan was to wait for a coming gladiatorial show. The advantage would be, because of the show, no suspicion would be aroused if arms were seen prepared for the attempt. But the majority opinion favoured killing him while he sat in the Senate, where he would be by himself since non-Senators would not be admitted, and where the many conspirators could hide their daggers beneath their togas. This plan won the day.

Character Profiles

Julius Caesar

Gaius Julius Caesar played a crucial role in transforming the Roman republic into the Roman Empire. His conquest of Gaul helped extend the Roman rule as far as the Atlantic ocean, and in return he expected political advancement in Rome. He proclaimed himself dictator-for-life and set about reforming Roman society, but Marcus Brutus and a group of senators wanted a return to the traditions of the Roman republic, and vowed to end Caesar's dictatorship.

Calpurnia Pisonis
(Caesar's third and last wife)

Calpurnia is not mentioned very often in ancient Roman texts, but it is known that she was the daughter of Lucius Piso, a statesman of Rome. Most historians are of the opinion that she was a strong and well-educated woman who was not generally given to superstition. Perhaps that is why Caesar was prepared to listen to her when, woken in the middle of the night by a howling gale, she told him of a terrible nightmare. She had dreamt that her house lay in ruins and she saw Caesar, her husband, mortally injured, and streaming with blood. Following the nightmare she tried desperately to convince her husband to postpone his meeting with the senate – but Brutus convinced him otherwise. Following her husband's death, Calpurnia delivered all his papers, including his will, as well as all his most precious possessions, to Mark Antony.

Brutus

Marcus Junius Brutus was a Roman senator in Caesar's senate. He was the son of Marcus Junius Brutus the elder and Servilia Caepionis, who went on to become a mistress of Caesar's. At the time there was much speculation that Caesar might have been Brutus's father, but this is unlikely, considering that Caesar was only 15 years old at the time of Brutus's birth. His affair with Brutus's mother did not begin until he was 25 years old. Nevertheless Caesar wanted to believe that Brutus was his son – and acted as a father towards him.

THE WITNESS'S ACCOUNT

His friends were alarmed at certain rumours and tried to stop him going to the Senate-house, as did his doctors, for he was suffering from one of his occasional dizzy spells. His wife, Calpurnia, especially, who was frightened by some visions in her dreams, clung to him and said that she would not let him go out that day. But Brutus, one of the conspirators who was then thought of as a firm friend, came up and said, 'What is this, Caesar? Are you a man to pay attention to a woman's dreams and the idle gossip of stupid men, and to insult the Senate by not going out, although it has honoured you and has been specially summoned by you? But listen to me, cast aside the forebodings of all these people, and come. The Senate has been in session waiting for you since early this morning.' This persuaded Caesar and he left.

Before he entered the chamber, the priests brought up the victims for him to make what was to be his last sacrifice. The omens were clearly unfavourable. After this unsuccessful sacrifice, the priests made repeated sacrifices, to see if anything more propitious might appear than what had already been revealed to them. In the end they said that they could not clearly see the divine intent, for there was some transparent, malignant spirit hidden in the victims. Caesar was annoyed and abandoned divination till sunset, though the priests continued all the more with their efforts.

Those of the murderers present were delighted at all of this, though Caesar's friends asked him to put off the meeting of the Senate for that day because of what the priests had said, and he agreed. But some attendants came up, calling him and saying that the Senate was full. He glanced at his friends, but Brutus approached him again and said, 'Come, good sir, pay no attention to the babblings of these men, and do not postpone what Caesar and his mighty power has seen fit to arrange. Make your own courage your favourable omen.' He persuaded Caesar with these words, took him by the right hand, and led him to the Senate which was quite near. Caesar followed in silence.

....

"Make your own courage your favourable omen"

....

The Senate rose in respect for his position when they saw him entering. Those who were to take part in the plot stood near him. Right next to him went Tillius Cimber, whose brother had been exiled by Caesar. Under pretext of a humble request on behalf of this brother, Cimber approached and grasped the mantle of his toga, seeming to want to make a more positive move with his hands upon Caesar. Caesar wanted to get up and use his hands, but was prevented by Cimber and became exceedingly annoyed.

That was the moment for the men to set to work. All quickly unsheathed their daggers and rushed at him. First Servilius Casca struck him with the point of the blade on the left shoulder a little above the collar-bone. He had been aiming for the throat, but in the excitement he missed. Caesar rose to defend himself, and in the uproar Casca shouted out in Greek to his brother. The latter heard him and drove his sword into the ribs. After a moment, Cassius made a slash at his face, and Decimus Brutus pierced him in the side. While Cassius Longinus was trying to give him another blow he missed and struck Marcus Brutus on the hand. Minucius also hit out at Caesar and hit Rubrius in the thigh. They were just like men doing battle against him.

Under the mass of wounds, he fell at the foot of Pompey's statue. Everyone wanted to seem to have had some part in the murder, and there was not one of them who failed to strike his body as it lay there until, wounded thirty-five times, he breathed his last.

DINNER WITH ATTILA THE HUN

A luxurious meal, served on silver plates, had been made ready for us and the barbarian guests

WITNESSED BY
PRISCUS

A deputation from the Western Roman emperor arrived in Scythia at the residence of Attila, the king of the Huns, to attempt to settle a dispute. Attila, who was much feared for his cruelty, was angry about a broken agreement concerning some gold vessels that were supposed to be supplied by a dealer called Constantius. The Western emperor sent a substantial embassy, consisting of Romulus, Promotus, Romanus and several other ambassadors, but Attila had Constantius crucified. Now he demanded that the Romans surrender to him for punishment a silver plate dealer called Silvanus as well. It was then that Maximin and Priscus travelled from Constantinople to Scythia to talk to Attila before he moved off to the North. They managed to get an initial interview with Attila. Then came Attila's personal invitation to dinner.

THE WITNESS

Priscus was a Greek writer, from the Eastern Empire, and the impression he gained of Attila was very different from the terrifying earlier image described by Ammianus Marcellinus, a Western Roman. Possibly Attila and his court had changed as result of contact with European courts; possibly the Western Romans had simply misrepresented him. Priscus remarked that Attila's residence in Scythia 'was more splendid than his houses in other places. It was made of polished boards and surrounded with wooden enclosures, not so much for protection as for the sake of appearance.'

THE WITNESS SETS THE SCENE

When we [Maximin and Priscus] returned to our tent, the father of Orestes came with an invitation from Attila for both of us to a banquet at three o'clock. When the hour arrived we went to the palace, along with the embassy from the Western

Romans, and stood on the threshold of the hall in the presence of Attila.

The cup-bearers gave us a cup, according to the national custom, that we might pray before we sat down.

Character Profiles

Priscus

Priscus was a diplomat, a sophist and a historian from Panium, in Thrace. He was the author of a historical work in eight books known as the Byzantine History, but only fragments of his manuscript remain. In addition to accompanying Maximin on his visit to the court of Attila the Hun, he also visited Arabia and Egypt, but it is this account of his dinner with Attila which has proved most useful to historians.

Attila The Hun

The Romans commonly referred to Attila the Hun as The Scourge of God. He was the leader of a kingdom centred around modern-day Hungary and, like the Romans themselves, adopted an expansionist foreign policy. He and his armies invaded any country they could in order to gain as much power and wealth as possible. Today most people think of Attila the Hun as an uncivilized and aggressive thug, and this is precisely what the Romans thought of him too. That is at least before Priscus showed him to be a more dignified statesman than they had previously imagined.

The Huns

The Huns were a confederation of nomadic, or semi nomadic equestrian tribes from central Asia and Europe. There is much debate about their specific origins, but historians generally agree that the Huns were not actually of one racial origin, but made up of lots of different Eurasian warrior-clans who identified themselves as 'Hun' because the name carried a certain prestige at the time. When Attila the Hun became their leader, his armies invaded places where the Roman empire was weakest, threatening much of Gaul (modern-day France).

THE WITNESS'S ACCOUNT

Having tasted from the cup, we proceeded to take our seats; all the chairs were ranged along the walls of the room on either side. Attila sat in the middle on a couch; a second couch was set behind him, and from it steps led up to his bed, which was covered with linen sheets and wrought coverlets for ornament, such as Greeks and Romans use to deck bridal beds. The places on the right of Attila were held chief in honour, those on the left, where we sat, were only second. Berichus, a noble among the Scythians, sat on our

DINNER WITH ATTILA THE HUN

side, but had the precedence of us. Onegesius sat
on a chair on the right of Attila's couch, and over
against Onegesius on a chair sat two of Attila's
sons; his eldest son sat on his couch, not near
him, but at the far end, with his eyes fixed on the
ground, in shy respect for his father. When all
were arranged, a cup-bearer came and handed
Attila a wooden cup of wine. He took it, and
saluted the first in precedence, who, honoured by
the salutation, stood up, and might not sit down
until the king, having tasted or drained the wine,
returned the cup to the attendant. All the guests
then honoured Attila in the same way, saluting
him, and then tasting the cups; but he did not
stand up. Each of us had a special cup-bearer,
who would come forward in order to present
the wine when the cup-bearer of Attila retired.
When the second in precedence and those next to
him had been honoured in the same way, Attila
toasted us according to the order of the seats.

When this ceremony was over the cup-bearers
retired and tables, large enough for three or more

to sit at, were placed next to the table of Attila, so that each could partake of the food on the dishes without leaving his seat. The attendant of Attila first entered with a dish full of meat, and behind him came the other attendants with bread and viands, which they laid on the tables. A luxurious meal, served on silver plates, had been made ready for us and the barbarian guests, but Attila ate nothing but meat on a wooden trencher.

In everything else, too, he showed himself temperate; his cup was made of wood, while the guests were given goblets of gold and silver. His dress, too, was quite simple, affecting only to be clean. The sword he carried at his side, the latchets of his Scythian shoes, the bridle of his horse were not adorned, like those of the other Scythians, with gold or gems or anything costly. When the viands of the first course had been consumed we all stood up, and did not resume our seats until each one, in the same order as before, drank to the health of Attila with the goblet of wine presented to him.

We then sat down, and a second dish was placed on each table with eatables of another kind. After this course the same ceremony was observed as after the first. When evening fell torches were lit, and two barbarians coming forward in front of Attila sang songs they had composed, celebrating his victories and deeds of valour in war. And of the guests, as they looked at the singers, some were pleased with the verses, others reminded of wars were excited in their souls, while yet others, whose bodies were feeble with age and their spirits compelled to rest, shed tears. After the songs a Scythian appeared whose mind was deranged, and by uttering outlandish and senseless words forced the company to laugh.

....

"nor by word or act did he betray anything approaching a smile of merriment"

....

After him Zerkon, the Moorish dwarf, entered. He had been sent by Attila as a gift to Aetius, and Edecon had persuaded him to come to Attila in order to recover his wife, whom he had left behind him in Scythia; the lady was a Scythian whom he had obtained in marriage through the influence of his patron Bleda. He did not succeed in recovering her, for Attila was angry with him for returning. On the occasion of the banquet he [Zerkon the dwarf] made his appearance, and threw all except Attila into fits of unquenchable laughter by his appearance, his dress, his voice and his words, which were a confused jumble of Latin, Hunnic, and Gothic. Attila, however, remained immovable and of unchanging countenance - nor by word or act did he betray anything approaching a smile of merriment except at the entry of Ernas, his youngest son, whom he pulled by the cheek, and gazed on with a calm look of satisfaction. I was surprised that he made so much of this son, and neglected his other children, but a barbarian who sat beside me and knew Latin, bidding me not reveal what he told, gave me to understand that prophets had forewarned Attila that his race would fall, but would be restored by this boy.

When the night had advanced we retired from the banquet, not wishing to drink any more.

THE BATTLE OF HASTINGS

The shouts both of the Normans and of the barbarians were drowned in the clash of arms and by the cries of the dying

WITNESSED BY
WILLIAM OF POITIERS

On 29 September, 1066, William, Duke of Normandy landed with an army at Pevensey Bay, Sussex, intent on claiming the throne of England. After erecting a prefabricated wooden castle at Hastings, the duke moved northwards. The English army of King Harold had just marched from the North after fending off another invasion attempt by the king of Norway, Harold Hardrada, who was defeated at the Battle of Stamford Bridge on 25 September. On 14 October, on the road north from Hastings, Duke William met King Harold. The two armies famously met at a place described rather strangely in the Anglo-Saxon Chronicle as 'the grey apple tree', the place that is now called Battle. The English army formed up on the ridge where Battle Abbey was later built, overlooking a valley to the south. The battle was a turning-point in English history, marking the Norman conquest and the end of the line of English (Saxon) kings.

THE WITNESS

There were no eye-witnesses at the Battle of Hastings who later wrote down what happened. The nearest thing to a witness is William of Poitiers, who was William the Conqueror's chaplain. He compiled an account of it from interviews with Norman soldiers who were there. His account is full but obviously biased. The only contemporary account of the battle written from the English point of view is a short description in the Anglo-Saxon Chronicle.

THE WITNESS SETS THE SCENE

The English took up their position on higher ground, on a hill abutting a forest through which they had just come. There, at once dismounting, they drew themselves up on foot and in very close order. The duke [William of Normandy] and his men, in no way dismayed by the difficulty of the ground, came slowly up the hill, and the terrible sound of trumpets on both sides signalled the beginning of the battle.

Character Profiles

William of Poitiers

William of Poitiers was considered by many to be the most well-informed man of his generation. He was born in Normandy around the year 1020, and studied in Poitiers before becoming a Norman knight and taking part in several battles. He eventually entered the priesthood, and it was during his posting as Archdeacon of Lisieux that he met and became friends with William, Duke of Normandy.

When William of Normandy became king of England in 1066, he invited his friend William of Poitiers to join him as his own personal chaplain. It was around this time that Poitiers decided to begin recording William's memoirs in his *'Life of William the Conqueror'*. or *'Gesta Guilelmi II, ducis Normannorum, regis Anglorum I'*.

William, Duke of Normandy

William of Normandy was born in 1027, the illegitimate son of Robert Duke of Normandy and Herleva of Falaise. Before setting out on a pilgrimage to the Holy Land in 1035, Robert of Normandy forced all his lords to swear fealty to William because, although he was illegitimate, he was Robert's only surviving son. When Harold ascended the throne of England, William of Normandy took it as a direct challenge and a deep personal insult. Two years previously Harold had sworn an oath of allegiance to William, though under duress, and Edward the Confessor had named William as the next king of England. William decided to take the throne, by force if necessary, and he quickly recruited an invasion force to sail for England.

Harold of Wessex

Harold Godwinson was born in about 1022, the son of a very powerful Anglo-Saxon, Earl

Godwin of Wessex. Harold had three brothers: Swegen, Tostig and Gyrth, as well as one sister: Edith, who was married to Edward the Confessor. When his father died, Harold inherited his titles – effectively becoming the most powerful man in England. He was favourite to succeed Edward as king, and was named as the king's successor on Edward's death bed. The trouble arose because Edward had previously promised the throne of England to William. In addition, Harold, under duress, had also promised to support William in his claim. Harold was nevertheless the legitimate heir to the childless Edward the Confessor, and William was the usurper.

THE WITNESS'S ACCOUNT

The eager boldness of the Normans gave them the advantage of attack. The Norman foot drawing nearer provoked the English by raining death and wounds upon them with their missiles. But the

English resisted valiantly, hurling back spears and javelins, axes, stones fastened to pieces of wood. . .The shouts both of the Normans and of the barbarians were drowned in the clash of arms and by the cries of the dying and for a long time the battle raged with the utmost fury. The English however had the advantage of the ground and profited by remaining in their position in close order. They gained further superiority from their numbers, from the impregnable front which they preserved and most of all from the manner in which their weapons found easy passage through the shields and armour of their enemies.

The foot-soldiers and Breton knights broke in flight before the English and also the troops on the left wing and the whole army of the duke was in danger of retreat. . . The Normans believed that their lord was killed. Seeing the hostile host pursuing his own troops, the prince thrust himself in front of those in flight, shouting at them and threatening them with his spear. He took off his helmet and cried, 'Look at me well. I am still alive. What is this madness which makes you fly? You are throwing away victory and lasting glory. And all for nothing since none of you can escape destruction.' He restored their courage. The Normans then surrounded several thousands of their pursuers and cut them down. Heartened by this success, they furiously carried their attack on to the main body of the English host...

Realizing that they could not overcome an army massed so strongly in close formation, the Normans feigned flight, for they recalled that a short while ago their flight had given them an advantage. The barbarians shouted with triumph. Several thousand of them, as before, gave rapid pursuit; but the Normans, suddenly wheeling their horses, surrounded them and cut them down. Twice this ruse was employed with the utmost success.

At last the English began to weary. The Normans threw and struck and pierced. Thus fortune crowned the triumph of William. . . He dominated this battle, checking his own men in flight, strengthening their spirit and sharing their dangers. Thrice his horse fell under him; thrice he avenged the death of his steed. His sharp sword pierced shields, helmets and armour. His knights seeing him thus fight on foot were filled with wonder and took new heart.

....

"Thrice his horse fell under him; thrice he avenged the death of his steed"

....

Evening was now falling and the English saw that they could not hold out much longer. They knew that they had lost a great part of their army, and they also knew that their king with two of his brothers [Earl Leofwine and Earl Gyrth] and many of their greatest men had fallen. They began to fly as swiftly as they could, some on horseback, some on foot, some along the roads, but most across the trackless country. Many left their corpses in the depths of the forest, and others were found by their pursuers lying by the roadside. The Normans eagerly carried on the pursuit and striking the rebels in the back brought a happy end to this famous victory. But some of those who retreated took courage to renew the struggle on more favourable ground, in a steep valley intersected with ditches. These people, descended from the ancient Saxons (the fiercest of men), are always by nature eager for battle, and they could only be brought down by greatest valour. Had they not recently defeated with ease the king of Norway at the head of a fine army?

The duke returned to the main battlefield and he could not gaze without pity on the carnage, although the slain were evil men, and although it is good and glorious in a just war to kill a tyrant. The bloodstained battle-ground was covered with the flower of the youth and nobility of England. The two brothers of the king were found near him, and Harold himself stripped of all badges of honour could not be identified by his face, but only by certain marks on his body. His corpse was brought into the duke's camp and William gave it to William, surnamed Malet, and not to Harold's mother, who offered for the body its weight in gold. For the duke thought it unseemly to receive money for such merchandise. Equally he considered it wrong that Harold should be buried as his mother wished, since so many men lay unburied because of his avarice. They said in jest that he who had guarded the coast with such insensate zeal should be buried by the seashore.

How was King Harold killed?

The Battle of Hastings is one of the most famous events in British history, but little is known for certain about the death of the last English King. Common knowledge has it that Harold was killed by an arrow in the eye, but there is no concrete evidence to back up this theory. Most contemporary historians of the time give no such detail. The Bayeux tapestry, was created soon after the Battle of Hastings and appears to show a soldier, thought to be Harold Godwinson, with an arrow in his eye. However, in the frame the soldier in question is standing up, he is neither on the ground nor falling to the ground, which indicates that he is not dead or wounded. The words above the frame read 'Hic Harold Rex Interfectus est', – 'Here King Harold has been Killed'. Most modern-day historians therefore conclude that King Harold is actually the man clearly falling to the ground on the right of the frame.

Mystery surrounds not only the death, but also the burial of Harold II. His final resting place has never been found. Traditional-ists believe that he was buried at Waltham Abbey in Essex – and this remains his official grave site. The historian John Pollock thinks that Harold was buried below the chancel arch at Holy Trinity Church in Bosham, West

Sussex. Others believe that Harold was buried at Senlac Hill, the ridge from which he deployed his men during the Battle of Hastings. William wanted him buried as his men were buried, as a bloody casualty of war, and not as a martyred king. This explains the secrecy behind Harold's death and the disposal of his remains.

THE MURDER OF THOMAS BECKET

The just, like a bold lion, shall be free from fear

WITNESSED BY
EDWARD GRIM

Thomas Becket, Archbishop of Canterbury, was murdered in his cathedral on 29 December 1170. There had been tension between Henry II, the king of England, and his chancellor, Thomas Becket, from the moment Henry insisted on making Thomas his Archbishop of Canterbury in 1162. A major power struggle between Church and state developed. While in France in December 1170, the king angrily goaded a group of barons into dealing with Thomas. Their response was to cross the Channel and ride to Canterbury, which they reached on 29 December. After an exchange of insults in the archbishop's palace, the barons armed themselves outside, followed Becket into the cathedral as he went to attend the vespers service, and murdered him in the north transept.

Henry II and the church

Henry II and Thomas Becket began their relationship as close friends and ended it as bitter enemies. The main disagreement between them, the one that led to Becket's murder, concerned the age-old power struggle between the church and the crown. When Becket became Archbishop of Canterbury, Henry assumed that his loyalties would stay where they always had been – firmly with the king. But Henry was gravely mistaken. When Thomas became archbishop his public persona underwent a significant and sudden change. He swapped his fine clothes for austere garments – choosing to wear a hair shirt beneath his vestments, and he regularly asked to be flogged by his staff as penance for his sins. He became extremely strict in his observance of church law, and he expounded the view that the power of the law of God, as laid down in the Bible, far excelled that of royal law, determined by the king. He was of the opinion that a priest should not be answerable to a court of law, but to the church courts and ultimately to God himself. Henry wanted to change

English law so that 'criminous clerks' were accountable to royal courts like everyone else. Henry II felt betrayed by Becket; he had expected loyalty from the man he had advanced. Like many others, including the bishops, Henry was unaware of Thomas's secret religious life, which had continued throughout his time as the king's chancellor.

THE WITNESS

Becket was accompanied by a group of monks and clerks, who were anxious for his safety. One was Edward Grim, a clerk from Cambridge who happened to be visiting Canterbury that day. In later images and accounts, Grim is depicted as Becket's cross-bearer, but this role was created for him subsequently for the sake of the symbolism. In a similar way, Grim describes Becket as suffering five wounds, just as Christ suffered five wounds. We have to bear the medieval emphasis on religious symbolism in mind when evaluating the narrative.

Four others in the cathedral at the time later wrote about what they saw: John of Salisbury, William FitzStephen, Benedict of Peterborough and William of Canterbury. But they all fled when Becket was attacked; only Grim stayed with him during the murder, nearly losing his own life trying to save the Archbishop. His arm was cut almost in two. Strange to say, virtually nothing is known about Edward Grim's life either before or after that dark December afternoon.

THE WITNESS SETS THE SCENE

When the holy archbishop entered the cathedral the monks stopped vespers and ran to their father, whom they had heard was dead, and saw that he was alive and unharmed. They hastened to close the doors of the church, but the great champion turned towards them and ordered the doors be thrown open. He said, 'It is not proper to turn a house of prayer, a church of Christ, into a fortress; even though it is not locked up, it is able to defend his people. We shall triumph over the enemy by suffering rather than by fighting - and we come to suffer, not to resist.'

Straight away the sacrilegious men entered with swords drawn; indeed the very sight of them, let alone the clanging of their arms, caused horror to those who watched. Everyone there was in tumult and fright, and those who had been singing vespers had now come to witness the dreadful scene. The knights approached the confused and disordered crowd and exclaimed in fury, 'Where is Thomas Becket, traitor to the king and realm?' He did not answer, so they immediately shouted out more loudly still, 'Where is the archbishop?'

Character Profiles

Thomas Becket

Thomas Becket was born in 1120, the son of a prosperous Norman merchant who had settled in London. He was educated in France and Italy and at Pevensey Castle before joining the staff of Theobald, the Archbishop of Canterbury. Theobald sent Becket on various missions to Rome, and his talents were noticed by the king of England, King Henry II. The two became great friends, Henry even named Becket as his chancellor. When Theobald died, Thomas Becket succeeded to the role of Archbishop of Canterbury. This irritated Becket's colleagues in the church because Becket had never been a priest. Once he was archbishop, he took his new responsibilities seriously. It soon became clear to Henry II that Becket was prepared to stand up for the church in any disagreement with the crown. Henry began to see Becket as a nuisance, and by 1170 the king had decided that he wanted Becket permanently out of the way.

King Henry II

Henry II was the first king of the Plantagenet family, also called the house of Anjou. He was born and raised in Anjou, France and did not make his first visit to England until 1142, when he came to defend his mother's, claim to the English throne.

Henry II has been called the most effective of all England's monarchs. He came to the throne in 1154 amid the anarchy of King Stephen's reign, and managed to restore order to the country by bringing to account all the errant barons, who had used Stephen's system of feudal law to undermine the king. He retrieved Cumbria and Northumbria from Malcolm IV of Scotland, and he refined the Norman system of government, creating a stable bureaucracy. It was dangerous to oppose Henry II, as his rebellious sons, as well as Thomas Becket, found out.

THE WITNESS'S ACCOUNT

Unshaken, he replied as it is written, 'The just, like a bold lion, shall be free from fear.' He descended from the steps to which he had been taken by the monks who were fearful of the knights and said in a clear voice, 'I am here, no traitor to the king but a priest. Why do you seek me?' The murderers followed him and asked, 'Absolve and restore to communion those you have excommunicated and return to office those you have suspended.'

He [Thomas] replied, 'No penance has been made, so I will not absolve them.'

Then now,' they said, 'you will die and get what you deserve.'

'And I,' he said, 'am prepared to die for my Lord, so that in my blood the church will attain liberty and peace; but in the name of Almighty God I forbid that you hurt my men, either cleric or layman, in any way.' The glorious martyr acted thoughtfully and with consideration for his men, so that no one near him would be hurt as he hastened toward Christ. 'If it is me you seek, let these people go on their way.'

Then they laid sacrilegious hands on him, pulling him and dragging him roughly so that they might kill him outside the walls of the church or carry him away as a prisoner, as they later confessed. But when it was not possible to move him easily from the pillar [in the middle of the north transept], one of the knights pressed on him and held onto him tightly. He [Thomas] bravely pushed him off, calling him a panderer and saying, 'Touch me not, Reginald. You owe me fealty and obedience. You and your accomplices are fools.'

Fired with a terrible rage the knight swung his sword over the sacred crown. He cried, 'I don't owe faith or obedience to you that is in opposition to the fealty I owe my lord king.' The unconquered martyr - seeing that the hour which would bring the end to his miserable mortal life was at hand and already promised by God to be the next to receive the crown of immortality - bent his neck as if in prayer and joined his hands and lifted them up. He commended himself and the cause of the Church to God, St Mary, and the blessed martyr St Denis.

Scarcely had he said these words when the wicked knight, fearing that he [Thomas] would be saved by the people and escape alive, leapt upon him suddenly and wounded this sacrificial lamb of God in the head, cutting off the top of his crown which the sacred unction of chrism had dedicated to God; and by the same blow he wounded the lower arm of him who tells this. Indeed he [Edward] stood firmly with the holy archbishop, holding him in his arms, when all the others, both clerics and monks, fled, and held him in his arms until the one he had raised in opposition to the blow was severed.

Then he received another blow on the head but still stood firm. But with the third the stricken martyr fell onto his knees and elbows, saying in a low voice, 'For the name of Jesus and the protection of the church I am ready to embrace death.' Then the third knight inflicted a terrible wound as he lay; with this blow he shattered the sword on the stone, and his crown was separated from his head so that the blood turned white from the brain yet no less did the brain turn red from the blood; it dyed purple the surface of the virgin mother church with the life and death of the confessor and martyr in the colours of the lily and the rose.

The fourth knight drove away those who were gathering so that the others could finish the murder more freely and boldly. The fifth - no knight but that cleric who had entered with the knights - so that a fifth blow might not be spared him who had imitated Christ in other things, placed his foot on the neck of the holy priest and, horrible to say, scattered his brains and blood across the pavement, calling out to the others, 'Let us away, knights; he will rise no more.'

During all these incredible events the martyr displayed the virtue of perseverance. Not even when struck did he utter a word, nor let out a cry or a sigh, or a sign signalling any kind of pain.

KUBLAI KHAN
IN BATTLE

Now might you behold such flights of arrows from this side and from that, that the whole heaven was canopied with them and they fell like rain

WITNESSED BY
MARCO POLO

In 1287 Marco Polo was allowed to accompany Kublai Khan on an expedition to destroy the forces of the Khan's uncle and rival, Nayan. Nayan had gathered an enormous army with the intention of overthrowing his nephew and seizing his huge empire. As soon as he heard about Nayan's rebellion, Kublai Khan marched quickly north at the head of an army 460,000 strong. By taking such swift action, he was able to surprise Nayan, who was encamped with his army in a shallow valley.

THE WITNESS

In 1271, the brothers Nicolo and Maffeo Polo, two adventurous Venetian merchants, set off on their second long journey overland to Kublai Khan's court, this time taking with them Nicolo's seventeen-year-old son Marco. When they met the Khan, Marco Polo impressed him with his intelligence and knowledge of language and he soon found himself employed as the Khan's emissary and political adviser. Marco Polo's description of his travels, written down on his return to Europe from notes compiled in the East, caused a sensation when they were published.

Some historians have questioned the truthfulness of Marco Polo's account. Why would the Khan have employed a European as an emissary when there must have been many in his empire with superior knowledge of its languages? Marco Polo probably exaggerated his importance to the Khan, but much of what he described rings true.

THE WITNESS'S ACCOUNT

What shall I say about it? When day had well broken, there was the Khan with all his host on a hill overlooking the plain where Nayan lay in his tent, in all security, without the slightest thought of any one coming there to do him harm. In fact, this confidence of his was such that he kept no vedettes [mounted sentries] whether in front or behind; for he knew nothing of the coming of the Great Khan, because all the approaches had been completely occupied as I told you. Moreover, the place was in a remote wilderness, more than thirty marches from the Court, though the Khan had made the distance in twenty, so eager was he to come to battle with Nayan.

And what shall I tell you next? The Khan was there on the hill, mounted on a great wooden bartizan [a defensive tower], which was carried by four well-trained elephants, and over him was hoisted his standard, so high aloft that it could be seen from all sides. His troops were ordered in armies of 30,000 men apiece; and most of the horsemen had a foot-soldier each armed with a lance set on the crupper behind him (for it was thus that the infantry-men were disposed); and the whole plain seemed to be covered with his forces. So it was that the Great Khan's army was arrayed for battle.

When Nayan and his people saw what had happened, they were thrown into confusion, and rushed to arm themselves. Nevertheless they made themselves ready in good style and formed their troops in an orderly manner. And when all were in battle array on both sides as I have told you, and nothing remained but to fall to blows, then might you have heard a sound arise of many instruments of music, and of the voices of the whole of the two hosts loudly singing. For this is a custom of the Tartars, that before they join battle they all unite in singing and playing on a certain two-stringed instrument of theirs, a thing right pleasant to hear. And so they continue in their array of battle, singing and playing in this pleasing manner, until the great Naccara [giant battle drum] of the Prince is heard to sound. As soon as that begins to sound the fight also begins on both sides; and in no case before the Prince's Naccara sounds dare any commence fighting.

So then, as they were singing and playing, though ordered and ready for battle, the great Naccara of the Great Khan began to sound. And that of Nayan also began to sound. And from then on the din of battle was heard loudly from this side and from that. And they rushed to work so doughtily with their bows and their maces, with their lances and swords, and with the arblasts [heavy crossbows] of the foot-soldiers, that it was a wondrous sight to see. Now might you behold such flights of arrows from this side and from that, that the whole heaven was canopied with them and they fell like rain. Now might you see on this side and on that so many cavalrymen and men-at-arms fall slain that the whole field seemed covered with them. From this side and from that such cries arose from the crowds of the wounded and dying that, had God thundered, you would not have heard Him! For fierce and furious was the battle, and no quarter was given.

" then might you have heard a sound arise of many instruments of music, and of the voices of the whole of the two hosts loudly singing "

But why should I make a long story of it? It was the most fierce and fearful battle that ever has been fought in our day. Nor have there ever been such forces in the field in actual fight, especially of horsemen, as were then engaged - for, taking both sides, there were not fewer than 760,000 horsemen, a mighty force! and that without reckoning the foot-soldiers. The battle endured with various fortune on this side and on that until noon. But at the last, by God's pleasure and the right that was on his side, the Great Khan had the victory, and Nayan lost the battle and was utterly routed. For the army of the Great Khan performed such feats of arms that Nayan and his host turned and fled. But this availed nothing for Nayan; for he and all the barons with him were taken prisoners, and had to surrender to the Khan with all their arms.

Now you must know that Nayan was a baptized Christian, and bore the cross on his banner; but this was of no avail to him, seeing how grievously he had done amiss in rebelling against his Lord. For he was the Great Khan's liegeman, and was bound to hold his lands of him like all his ancestors before him.

THE BATTLE OF BANNOCKBURN

'Bannockburn' was a name on all English lips for many years to come

WITNESSED BY
THE MONK AT LANERCOST
AND SIR THOMAS GREY

The English king, Edward II, inherited an ongoing war against Scotland from his father, Edward I. Edward I was a strong king and a great war leader; his son was neither. Edward II was unpopular with the aristocracy because of his unaristocratic interests. He was interested in rustic pursuits such as digging ditches, gardening and thatching, and consequently earned for himself the contempt of fellow-aristocrats. He also had favourites, to whom he gave far too much power – first Piers Gaveston, then the Despensers, father and son. Edward II's behaviour at the Battle of Bannockburn which, apart from anything else, he should have won, did nothing to improve his popularity.

The Battle of Bannockburn was fought on 24 June 1314, on the broad floodplain of the River Forth in the Scottish lowlands, close to Stirling. The English king, Edward II, led an army into Scotland that was three times the size of the Scottish army led by Robert the Bruce.

THE WITNESSES

1) The author of this account was an anonymous monk at Lanercost Abbey in Cumbria. Probably the monk saw Edward II and his army at close quarters as it passed on its way to Scotland, but he did not actually see the battle. Instead, as he clearly says, his account relies on a report from someone who was there. Edward I, who is praised by the monk, is known to have visited Lanercost. The criticism levelled at Edward II implies that Edward II may also have visited Lanercost and been less generous to the monks. This might in turn introduce an element of bias into the account generally.

2) Sir Thomas Grey of Heton (1272-1363) was the son of an English soldier-knight of the same name who fought at the Battle of Bannockburn. Grey wrote his *Scalacronica* while imprisoned in Edinburgh Castle after being captured in a minor skirmish in 1355. The work is an ambitious history which includes a detailed account of

Bannockburn which he clearly got from his father.

THE WITNESSES' ACCOUNTS

1) The Lanercost Monk

In early May, the king of England approached the Scottish March [border] with a fine and mighty army. Yet whereas his father, Edward I, when going to war with the Scots, had been accustomed to visit the shrines of English saints and to make splendid offerings to them, Edward II rode along in great pomp with elaborate trappings, took goods from the monasteries and, so it is reported, said and did much that was harmful to the shrines.

In June, King Edward II gathered his forces together and approached Stirling Castle in great might, in order to break up the siege and to do battle with the Scots, who had assembled there with their entire strength. On 23 June, after midday, the English forces reached Tor Wood. The Scots, who were in the wood, fell upon the leading column of Robert Clifford's force, killing a number of men and forcing the rest to flee. After this incident, the English grew fearful, while the Scots became bolder.

....

"the great English horses rushed on to the Scottish pikes, which bristled like a dense forest"

....

When the two armies had drawn much closer to each other, all the Scots fell to their knees, saying the Lord's Prayer, commending themselves to God's protection and seeking divine assistance. This done, they marched boldly against the English. The Scottish army was drawn up with the first two lines each a little ahead of the one next to it, so that no line was in front of another. Robert Bruce was in the third and final line.

When the two armies joined battle, the great English horses rushed on to the Scottish pikes, which bristled like a dense forest. An appalling din arose from the splintering pikes and the warhorses, mortally wounded. This brought matters to a standstill for a while. The English could not pass the Scots' front line in order to reach the enemy; indeed they could do nothing to improve their situation, and their only recourse was to flight. I heard the tale of these events from a trustworthy eye-witness.

In the fighting in the front line, the dead included Gilbert of Clare, Earl of Gloucester, Robert Clifford and many other nobles, besides a great number of foot-soldiers.

Yet another misfortune befell the English, who had a little earlier crossed a deep ditch, a tidal inlet called the Bannock Burn; now as they struggled to retreat in confusion many noblemen and others fell into this ditch in the crush, along with their horses. Some managed to scramble out, but many were completely unable to extricate themselves. 'Bannockburn' was a name on all English lips for many years to come.

The king, with Hugh Despenser, who had become the apple of the king's eye after Piers Gaveston, and numerous English cavalry and infantry, were guided away by a Scottish knight who knew an escape route. Thus, to their eternal shame, they fled wretchedly to the castle at Dunbar. Some stragglers were killed by the Scots, who were in hot pursuit. From Dunbar, the king and a few of his closest companions took a boat to Berwick upon Tweed, leaving the rest to their fate.

2) Sir Thomas Grey

King Edward planned an expedition to these parts where, in attempting the relief of the castle of Stirling, he was defeated and a great number of people were slain, [including] the Earl of Gloucester and other right noble persons; and the Earl of Hereford was taken at Bothwell, to which he had retreated and where he was betrayed by the governor.

Robert the Bruce marched in force before the castle of Stirling, where Philip de Moubray, knight, having command of the said castle for the King of England, made terms with Robert the Bruce to surrender the said castle which he [Robert] had besieged unless he [de Moubray] should be relieved. That is, unless the English came within three leagues of the castle within eight days of St Johns Day in the summer next to come, he [de Moubray] would surrender the castle [to Robert]. The King of England came there for that reason [to ensure that Philip did not hand over Stirling to Robert the Bruce]. Philip met him [Edward II] at three leagues from the castle on Sunday the vigil of St John and told him there was no need to approach nearer, for he considered himself relieved. Then Philip told the King how the enemy had blocked the narrow roads in the forest.

The young troops would by no means stop but held their way[1]. The advanced guard, of which the Earl of Gloucester held command, entered

1 – They carried on.

the road within the Park, where they were immediately received roughly by the Scots who occupied the passage. Here Perris de Mountforth, knight, was slain with an axe by the hand of Robert the Bruce.

THE MURDER OF EDWARD II

As this brave knight was overcome, he shouted aloud so that many heard his cry both within and without the castle and knew it was the cry of a man who suffered a violent death

WITNESSED BY
GEOFFREY LE BAKER

Edward II antagonized his barons by giving too much power to his favourites. He antagonized his wife, Queen Isabella, with his homosexual love affairs. She cultivated a relationship with Roger Mortimer, a rebel whom Edward had imprisoned in the Tower. She probably engineered his escape and together they plotted Edward's overthrow. They forced his abdication on 25 January 1327, then arranged his murder in Berkeley Castle eight months later.

THE WITNESS

The account is by Geoffrey le Baker – and he begins by explaining that he is the mouthpiece of an eye-witness to the murder. 'These things were told me by William Bishop, in the time after the great plague[1]. He had seen them with his own eyes, for he had been among those who took Edward to Berkeley.'

Geoffrey le Baker evidently has some sort of personal agenda. He is very keen to heap blame

1 – The Black Death of 1348-49.

on the bishop of Hereford[2], for his role in the murder, yet he studiously avoids naming the actual murderers. The likeliest candidates are Lord Maltravers, Sir Thomas Gourney and William Ogle. There is no record of the eventual fate of Gourney and Ogle, though they did flee from England after the assassination. Maltravers, who rode to London to tell the queen that the deed was done, found himself accused and arrested. He was acquitted of Edward's murder, but later, almost incredibly, he was executed for committing a similar crime elsewhere.

THE WITNESS'S ACCOUNT

Finally they arrived at Berkeley Castle, where, ever patient in the face of his misfortunes, the noble Edward was shut up like a hermit. He was robbed of his earthly kingdom and stripped bare like the blessed Job, not by his rivals but by his own wife. Isabella was angered that his life which had become most hateful to her should be prolonged.

2 – Thomas Charleton, who became Lord Treasurer.

She asked advice of the bishop of Hereford, pretending that she had had a dreadful dream from which she feared that her husband would at some time be restored to his former dignity and would condemn her, as a traitress, to be burned or to perpetual slavery. The bishop feared greatly for himself, just as Isabella did, conscious as he was that he was guilty of treason.

And so letters were written to Edward's keepers, setting forth in vivid detail the false accusation that they had been too lenient with him and fed him on delicacies. Moreover, it was hinted that the death of Edward would cause these nobles no great displeasure, whether it were natural or violent. Concerning the point, the bishop of Hereford penned a message of double meaning: *'Edwardum occidere nolite timere bonum est.'* This saying may be resolved into two parts. The first consists of the first three words of the bishop's puzzle: *'Edwardum occidere nolite'* – *'Do not kill Edward!'* – followed by the second three: *'timere bonum est'* – Fear is a good thing.' Read thus, the message could not be construed as treason.

But those who received the message were aware of the true import of the bishop's communication. They construed the message thus: *'Edwardum occidere nolite timere* – 'Do not be afraid to kill Edward!' – followed by *'bonum est'* – 'It is good!' Those who were guilty of evil, read the message as evil. Thus did that skilful trickster [the bishop of Hereford] have recourse to a puzzle, for he knew that without his authority, Edward's keepers would not dare to carry out their cruel instructions and kill him, lest they should be brought to trial for this crime. The message made the bishop safe from any accusation of treason. Events were to prove the bishop correct.

In the end, Edward's murderers, who had believed that the favour of Isabella and the slippery and deceitful bishop made them secure, found that instead these two were eager to take vengeance for the murder of their hostage, Edward.

The keepers were dumbfounded and did not

know what to do. They showed the letters with the seals of Isabella, the bishop of Hereford and other conspirators to prove that the latter had indeed given their consent.

The bishop did not deny the letter, agreeing that he and his accomplices had sent it, but he explained it as being perfectly innocent and loyal in its meaning. It was the keepers, he claimed, who had misinterpreted it and used it as authority for their wicked deed. He so terrified them with his threats that they fled.

Edward II was welcomed kindly at the castle and treated well by Thomas Berkeley, lord of the estate. After receipt of the letter, Edward's torturers took control. They gave orders that Thomas Berkeley was to have no contact with Edward. This caused him not only sadness but shame for he was unable to do as he wished. Sighing, he bade Edward farewell and moved to another of his estates.

Then began the most extreme part of Edward's

persecutions. First, he was shut up in a secure chamber, where he was tortured for many days until he was almost suffocated by the stench of corpses buried in a cellar hollowed out beneath. But when his tyrannous warders perceived that the stench alone was not sufficient to kill him, they seized him on the night of 22 September as he lay sleeping in his room. There, with cushions[3] heavier than fifteen strong men could carry, they held him down, suffocating him.

Then they thrust a plumber's soldering iron, heated red hot, guided by a tube inserted into his bowels, and thus they burnt his innards and his vital organs. They feared lest, if he were to receive a wound in those parts of the body where generally men are wounded, it might be discovered by some man who honoured justice, and his torturers might be found guilty of manifest treason and made to suffer the consequent penalty.

As this brave knight was overcome, he shouted aloud so that many heard his cry both within and

3 – An unusual use of the word 'cushions'. Weights may be intended.

without the castle and knew it was the cry of a man who suffered a violent death. Many in both the town and castle of Berkeley were moved to pity for Edward, and to watch and pray for his spirit as it departed this world.

THE VOYAGE TO AMERICA

Arrived on shore, they saw trees very green, many streams of water, and diverse sorts of fruits

WITNESSED BY
CHRISTOPHER COLUMBUS

Columbus and his men famously sailed across the North Atlantic in the summer of 1492 to discover North America in three small ships, the *Pinta*, the *Nina* and his flagship, the *Santa Maria*.

THE WITNESS

These are extracts from the diary of Christopher Columbus. In it he refers to himself formally in the third person as 'the Admiral'. It is interesting to see Columbus systematically lying to his crew, telling them that they had sailed a shorter distance westwards for fear of frightening them. Had he also lied about where they were going?

THE WITNESS'S ACCOUNT

6 August. The rudder of the caravel[1] *Pinta* became loose. It was believed that this happened by the contrivance of Gomez Rascon and Christopher Quintero, who were on board the caravel, because they disliked the voyage.

1 – A small ship with lateen (triangular) sails.

9 August. At Grand Canary, [they] with much labour repaired the *Pinta*. They saw a great eruption of flames from the Peak of Tenerife, a lofty mountain. The *Pinta*, which before had carried lateen sails, they altered and made her square-rigged.

9 September. Sailed this day nineteen leagues[2], and determined to count less than the true number, that the crew might not be dismayed if the voyage should prove long. In the night sailed thirty leagues.

10 September. This day and night sailed sixty leagues. Reckoned only forty-eight leagues.

16 September. Sailed day and night, west thirty-nine leagues, and reckoned only thirty-six. Here they began to meet with large patches of weeds very green, and which appeared to have been recently washed away from the land; on which account they all judged themselves to be near some island, though not a continent, according to the opinion of the Admiral, who says, 'The

2 – A league is three miles.

continent we shall find further ahead.'

17 September. Steered west and sailed, day and night, above fifty leagues; wrote down only forty-seven. At dawn they saw many more weeds, apparently river weeds and among them a live crab, which the Admiral kept, and says that these are sure signs of land, being never found eighty leagues out at sea. They found the sea-water less salt since they left the Canaries, and the air milder.

19 September. Continued, and sailed, day and night, twenty-five leagues, experiencing a calm. Wrote down twenty-two. This day at ten o'clock a pelican came on board, and in the evening another; these birds are not accustomed to go twenty leagues from land.

25 September. Very calm this day; At sunset Martin Alonzo called out with great joy from his vessel that he saw land, and demanded of the Admiral a reward for his intelligence. The Admiral says, when he heard him declare this, he fell on his knees and returned thanks to God, and Martin Alonzo with his crew repeated *Gloria in excelsis Deo*, as did the crew of the Admiral. Those on board the *Nina* ascended the rigging and all declared they saw land. The Admiral also thought it was land, and about twenty-five leagues distant.

26 September. Discovered that what they had taken for land was nothing but clouds. Sailed, day and night, thirty-one leagues; reckoned to the crew twenty-four.

6 October. Continued their course west and sailed forty leagues day and night; reckoned to the crew thirty-three. Martin Alonzo gave it as his opinion that they had better steer from west to southwest. The Admiral thought from this that Martin Alonzo did not wish to proceed onward to Cipangu[3]; but he considered it best to keep on his course, as he should probably reach the land sooner in that direction, preferring to visit the continent[4] first, and then the islands.

3 – Cipangu was the medieval Chinese name for Japan.
4 – By implication the mainland of eastern Asia: China.

> " *Sailed this day nineteen leagues, and determined to count less than the true number, that the crew might not be dismayed if the voyage should prove long. In the night sailed thirty leagues.* "

7 October. Continued their course west and sailed twelve miles an hour, for two hours, then eight miles an hour. Sailed till an hour after sunrise, twenty-three leagues; reckoned to the crew eighteen. At sunrise the caravel *Nina*, who kept ahead on account of her swiftness in sailing, while all the vessels were striving to outsail one another, and gain the reward promised by the King and Queen by first discovering land - hoisted a flag at her mast head, and fired a lombarda[5], as a signal that she had discovered land, for the Admiral had given orders to that effect. He had

5 – The same as a bombard, an early type of cannon.

also ordered that the ships should keep in close company at sunrise and sunset, as the air was more favourable at those times for seeing at a distance. Towards evening seeing nothing of the land which the *Nina* had made signals for, and observing large flocks of birds coming from the North and making for the southwest, whereby it was rendered probable that they were either going to land to pass the night, or abandoning the countries of the north, on account of the approaching winter, he determined to alter his course, knowing also that the Portuguese had discovered most of the islands they possessed by attending to the flight of birds. The Admiral accordingly shifted his course from west to west-southwest, with a resolution to continue two days ill that direction. This was done about an hour after sunset. Sailed in the night nearly five leagues, and twenty-three in the day. In all twenty-eight.

10 October. Steered west-southwest; day and night made fifty-nine leagues' progress; reckoned to the crew but forty-four. Here the men lost all patience, and complained of the length of the voyage.

11 October. Steered west-southwest; and encountered a heavier sea than they had met with before in the whole voyage. The crew of the *Pinta* saw a cane and a log; they also picked up a stick which appeared to have been carved with an iron tool, a piece of cane, a plant which grows on land, and a board. The crew of the *Nina* saw other signs of land, and a stalk loaded with rose berries. These signs encouraged them, and they all grew cheerful. The Admiral held it for certain that land was near; the Admiral directed them to keep a strict watch and look out diligently for land, and to him who should first discover it he promised a silken jacket, besides the reward which the King and Queen had offered.

At two o'clock in the morning the land was discovered, at two leagues' distance; they took in sail and remained under the square-sail, lying to until day, when they found themselves near a small island.[6] Presently they saw people, naked. The Admiral landed in the boat along with Martin Alonzo Pinzon and Vincent Yanez his brother, captain of the *Nina*. The Admiral bore the royal standard, and the two captains each a banner of the Green Cross, which all the ships had carried. Arrived on shore, they saw trees very green, many streams of water, and diverse sorts of fruits.

6 – It is still uncertain which island this was.

SIR THOMAS MORE

He has a fair skin, his complexion glowing rather than pale, though far from ruddy, but for a very faint rosiness shining through

WITNESSED BY
DESIDERIUS ERASMUS

Thomas More (1478-1535) was Lord Chancellor in the reign of Henry VIII. He was a pious, philosophical, scholarly man who became a great statesman and ultimately came to grief over a matter of principle. He was opposed to Henry VIII's divorce from Katherine of Aragon and after this clash of wills Henry VIII had him executed for treason.

THE WITNESS

More's great friend, both as a young man and in middle age, was Desiderius Erasmus, the Dutch scholar who was one of the leading figures in the North European Renaissance. When they were young men, an intense friendship developed between them. More was on his second marriage in 1519; Erasmus never married. At times in his description, Erasmus seems to be keening for the young man who was beyond his reach.

Erasmus dedicated his masterpiece, *In Praise of Folly*, to More. He described Thomas More in this letter to a German knight, Ulrich von Hutten. The letter was written in Antwerp and dated 23 July 1519.

Character Profiles

Sir Thomas More

Sir Thomas More was born in Milk Street in London on 7 February, 1478, the son of Sir John More – a prominent British lawyer. As a young man, More attended St Anthony's school in London before joining the staff of Archbishop Morton as a page. The archbishop noticed the young man's fine mind and predicted that Thomas would become 'a marvellous man'. He went on to study Latin and Greek at Oxford under the scholars Thomas Linacre and William Grocyn, before returning to London to become a barrister. Thomas was torn between entering the church or pursuing a career in politics. He was a devoutly religious man, and while he was studying to become a lawyer he also subjected himself to the hardships of a Carthusian monastic life. The habits of penance, fasting and prayer stayed with him for the rest of his life, but an illustrious political career beckoned and so he entered parliament. More met and became friends with the radical Catholic theologian Erasmus in 1499, when the latter was visiting England. The two quickly became life-long friends and regular correspondents. More's devout religion eventually led to his death, when Henry VIII divorced Katherine of Aragon and denounced the Pope, Thomas refused to recognize the split and so Henry VIII had him executed on Tower Hill on charges of treason.

....

Desiderius Erasmus
Desiderius Erasmus was born Gerrit Gerritszoon, the son of a priest in Rotterdam on 28 October in the late 1460s (the actual year of

his birth is unknown – but it is thought to have been 1466 or 1469). Little is known about his parentage, but it is very likely that he was illegitimate. Despite this less than ideal start in life he was well cared for by his parents and well educated. He was ordained in 1492 and studied in Paris. From 1499 onwards he lived the life of an independent scholar, moving from place to place teaching, lecturing and corresponding with European thinkers of the day. In 1500 he began writing on all subjects: religious and secular, and in 1509 he published 'In Praise of Folly', for his close friend Thomas More, to whom he was devoted.

THE WITNESS'S ACCOUNT

To begin with that side of More of which you know nothing, in height and stature he is not tall, nor again noticeably short, but there is such symmetry in all his limbs as leaves nothing to be desired here. He has a fair skin, his complexion glowing rather than pale, though far from ruddy, but for a very faint rosiness shining through. His hair is of a darkish blond, or if you will, a lightish brown, his beard scanty, his eyes bluish grey, with flecks here and there. . . His expression corresponds to his character, always showing a pleasant and friendly gaiety, and rather set in a smiling look; and to speak honestly better suited to merriment than to seriousness and solemnity, though far removed from silliness and buffoonery.

His right shoulder seems a little higher than the left, particularly when he is walking: this is not natural to him but due to force of habit, like many of the little habits which we pick up. There is nothing to strike one in the rest of his body; only his hands are somewhat clumsy, but only when compared with the rest of his appearance. He has always from a boy been very careless of everything to do with personal adornment, to the point of not greatly caring for those things which according to Ovid's teaching should be the sole care of men. One can tell even now, from his appearance in maturity, how handsome he must have been as a young man; although when I first knew him he was not more than three and twenty years old, for he is now barely forty.

His health is not so much robust as satisfactory, but equal to all the tasks becoming to an honourable citizen: there is every prospect of his living long, as he has a father of great age – but a wondrously fresh and green old age. I have never yet seen anyone less fastidious in his choice of food. Until he grew up he liked to drink water; in this he took after his father. But so as to avoid irritating anyone over this, he would deceive his comrades by drinking from a pewter pot ale that was very nearly all water. Wine – the custom in England is to invite each other to drink from the same goblet – he would often sip with his lips, not to give the appearance of disliking it, and at the same time to accustom himself to common ways.

He preferred beef, salt fish and bread of the second quality, well risen, to the foods commonly regarded as delicacies. Otherwise he was by no means averse from all sources of innocent pleasure, even to the appetite. He has always had a great liking for milk foods and fruit: he enjoys eating eggs.

His voice is neither strong nor at all weak, but easily audible, by no means soft or melodious but the voice of a clear speaker: for he seems to have no gift for vocal music, although he delights in every kind of music. His speech is wonderfully clear and distinct, with no trace of haste or hesitation.

He likes to dress simply, and does not wear silk or purple or gold chains, excepting where it would not be decent not to wear them.

In social intercourse he is of so rare a courtesy and charm of manners that there is no man so melancholy that he does not gladden, no subject so forbidding that he does not dispel the tedium of it. From his boyhood he has loved joking, so that he might seem born for this, but in his jokes he has never descended to buffoonery, and has never loved the biting jest.

In human relations he looks for pleasure in everything he comes across, even in the gravest matters. If he has to do with intelligent and educated men, he takes pleasure in their brilliance; if with the ignorant and foolish, he enjoys their folly. He is not put out by perfect fools, and suits himself with marvellous dexterity to all men's feelings. For women generally, even for his wife, he has nothing but jests and merriment.

....

"In social intercourse he is of so rare a courtesy and charm of manners that there is no man so melancholy that he does not gladden "

....

He takes an especial pleasure in watching the appearance, character and behaviour of various creatures. Accordingly, there is almost no kind of bird which he does not keep at his home, and various other animals not commonly found, such as apes, foxes, ferrets, weasels and their like. Added to this, he eagerly buys anything foreign which comes his way, and he has the whole house stocked with these objects, so that wherever the visitor looks there is something to detain him; and his own pleasure is renewed whenever he sees others enjoying these sights.

He diligently cultivates true piety, while being remote from all superstitious observance. He has set hours in which he offers to God not the customary prayers but prayers from the heart. With his friends he talks of the life of the world to come so that one sees that he speaks sincerely and not without firm hope. Such is More even at Court. And then there are those who think that Christians are to be found only in monasteries!

The court of Henry VIII

Henry VIII became king of England in 1509, the same year that Erasmus published his 'In Praise of Folly' for his great friend Sir Thomas More. Henry VIII's court consisted of 1,000 people. At this time people judged each other's importance according to how many attendants they had, so European monarchs attempted to out-do each other with bigger and more elaborate entourages in order to prove their superior magnificence and power. When Henry VIII met Francis I in Calais in 1520, a complete town of timber and tents had to be built in order to accommodate both kings and their various staff members. Vast amounts of velvet, satin and gold cloth were used to decorate temporary spaces in what became known as the 'field of the cloth of gold'. Quantity of servants was not the only important factor, quality was very important too – this explains why so many of

Henry's courtiers, attendants and servants came from other noble families. These boys were expected to play musical instruments, sing beautifully and compose music, read and discuss literature, speak several languages, wrestle, hunt, play tennis and joust. Thomas More was a Roman Catholic intellectual, and one of the most highly respected scholars of his day. He eventually came to the attention of the king, and Henry VIII sent him to the Spanish Netherlands as a commercial ambassador in 1515. In 1518 the king made More a member of the king's council and later, in 1521, he was knighted. The two became close allies, and Henry used his political power to install More as speaker of the house. However, this relationship was not to last, because the king was about to challenge one of More's fundamental beliefs: the idea of the pope as divine head of the church.

THE EXECUTION OF MARY QUEEN OF SCOTS

So perish all the Queen's enemies

WITNESSED BY
ROBERT WINKFIELDE

Mary Stuart fled from her kingdom in 1567 after a revolt by her barons. She went into voluntary exile in England, throwing herself on the mercy of her cousin, Elizabeth I, who did not welcome her presence. Mary was kept under close surveillance at a series of mansions, and finally confined to Fotheringhay Castle. As a Catholic alternative to the Protestant Elizabeth, she was naturally a focus for subversion and rebellion. Elizabeth's ministers wanted Mary disposed of; while she lived, Elizabeth was in danger. It was only when Mary was incriminated in the Babington Plot to overthrow and assassinate Elizabeth that the English queen agreed that Mary should be brought to trial. She remained ambivalent about the death sentence for Mary, because she had been similarly incriminated by others as a young woman herself, only narrowly avoiding execution.

Mary was beheaded in the great hall at Fotheringhay Castle on 8 February 1587. Her death as a 'Catholic martyr' gave Philip of Spain, another Catholic monarch, the pretext he wanted to invade England.

THE WITNESS

The witness was Robert Winkfielde, and he wrote his account specifically to send to William Cecil, Lord Burghley. When Burghley received this report, he wrote on it in his own handwriting, 'The Manner of the Q. of Scotts death at Fodringhay, wr. by Ro. Wy.'

THE WITNESS SETS THE SCENE

Her [Mary Queen of Scots] prayers being ended, the executioners, kneeling, desired her Grace to forgive them her death: who answered, 'I forgive you with all my heart, for now, I hope, you shall make an end of all my troubles.' Then they, with her two women, helping her up, began to disrobe her of her apparel: then she, laying her crucifix upon the stool, one of the executioners took from her neck the *Agnus Dei*, which she, laying hands off it, gave to one of her women and told the executioner he should be answered money for it. Then she suffered them, with her two women, to disrobe her of her chain of pomander beads and all other her apparel most willingly, and with joy rather than sorrow, helped to make unready herself, putting on a pair of sleeves with her own hands which they had pulled off, and that with some haste, as if she had longed to be gone.

All this time they were pulling off her apparel, she never changed her countenance, but with smiling cheer she uttered these words, 'that she never had such grooms to make her unready, and that she never put off her clothes before such a company.'

Then she, being stripped of all her apparel saving her petticoat and kirtle, her two women beholding her made great lamentation, and crying and crossing themselves prayed in Latin. She, turning herself to them, embracing them, said these words in French, *'Ne crie vous, j'ay promé pour vous'*, and so crossing and kissing them, bade them pray for her and rejoice and not weep, for that now they should see an end of all their mistress's troubles.

Character Profiles

Mary Queen of Scots

Mary Queen of Scots was born at Linlithgow Palace, Scotland, in 1542. Her father, James V of Scotland, died just six days after her birth, leaving her as infant successor to the crown of Scotland. Her French mother, Mary of Guise, became regent and she sent the young queen to France to grow up in the French royal household. In 1558, at the age of 16, Mary was married to the Dauphin Francis. He eventually succeeded to the French throne, making Mary queen of France and Scotland. In addition to this, many English

Catholics recognized Mary as rightful queen of England, because Elizabeth I was a protestant. Elizabeth knew that her position was precarious. In fact, Mary's lack of discretion in Scotland – her unwise marriage to Darnley and her reckless liaison with Bothwell – led to her downfall. She ended up seeking refuge in England, putting herself under Elizabeth's protection.

....

Elizabeth I

Elizabeth I was born in 1533 at Greenwich Palace to King Henry VIII and his second wife, Anne Boleyn. Her birth has been described as the greatest disappointment of her father's life. He had divorced his first wife, Katherine of Aragon, largely because of her failure to produce a male heir to the throne and then his new wife, Anne, also gave birth to a baby girl. Perhaps this feeling of disappointment influenced the young Elizabeth and helped to turn her into the tough and determined monarch she became. Her father's dynastic problems probably coloured her view of marriage, and helped her decide never to marry. Elizabeth did not delight in the downfall of her cousin. She saw her execution as a necessary evil.

THE WITNESS'S ACCOUNT

Then she, with a smiling countenance, turning to her men servants, as Melvin and the rest, standing upon a bench nigh the scaffold, who sometime weeping, sometime crying out aloud, and continually crossing themselves, prayed in Latin, crossing them with her hand bade them farewell, and wishing them to pray for her even until the last hour.

This done, one of the women having a *Corpus Christi* cloth lapped up three-corner-ways, kissing it, put it over the Queen of Scots' face, and pinned it fast to the caule[1] of her head. Then the two

1 – The back part of a woman's cap or hairnet.

women departed from her, and she kneeling down upon the cushion most resolutely, and without any token or fear of death, she spake aloud this Psalm in Latin, *In Te Domine confido, non confundar in eternam*. Then, groping for the block, she laid down her head, putting her chin over the block with both her hands, which, holding there still, had been cut off had they not been espied. Then lying upon the block most quietly, and stretching out her arms cried, *In manus tuas, Domine*, three or four times. Then she, lying very still upon the block, one of the executioners holding her slightly with one of his hands, she endured two strokes of the other executioner with an axe, she making very small noise or none at all, and not stirring any part of her from the place where she lay: and so the executioner cut off her head, saving one little gristle, which being cut asunder, he lift up her head to the view of all the assembly and bade *God save the Queen*. Then, her dress of lawn[2] falling from off her head, it appeared as grey as one of threescore and ten years old, polled[3] very short,

2 – Fine linen.
3 – Cropped or clipped.

her face in a moment being so much altered from the form she had when she was alive, as few could remember her by her dead face. Her lips stirred up and down a quarter of an hour after her head was cut off.

Then Mr Dean [Dr Fletcher, Dean of Peterborough] said with a loud voice, 'So perish all the Queen's enemies,' and afterwards the Earl of Kent came to the dead body, and standing over it, with a loud voice said, 'Such end of all the Queen's and the Gospel's enemies.'

....

"and so the executioner cut off her head, saving one little gristle, which being cut asunder, he lift up her head to the view of all the assembly and bade God save the Queen"

....

Then one of the executioners, pulling off her garters, espied her little dog which was crept under her clothes, which could not be gotten forth but by force, yet afterward would not depart from the dead corpse, but came and lay between her head and her shoulders, which being imbrued with her blood was carried away and washed, as all things else were that had any blood was either burned or washed clean, and the executioners sent away with money for their fees, not having any one thing that belonged unto her. And so, every man being commanded out of the hall, except the sheriff and his men, she was carried by them up into a great chamber lying ready for the surgeons to embalm her.

Elizabeth and Mary

The relationship between Elizabeth and Mary had always been very difficult. Elizabeth's position as queen of England was threatened by Mary who was seen by most

Catholics as the rightful queen of England. They refused to recognize the legitimacy of Henry VIII's marriage to Elizabeth's mother, Anne Boleyn, and so regarded Elizabeth as a child conceived out of wedlock. Illegitimate children were not viable heirs to the throne. Mary agreed with her fellow Catholics that Elizabeth was not the rightful queen of England. She believed that the crown belonged to her, and occasionally she referred to herself as the queen of England in exile, which must have annoyed and angered Elizabeth intensely. It seems bizarre given the obvious tensions which existed between these cousins, but for reasons of diplomacy they attempted to maintain the pretence of friendship. Mary was nine years older than Elizabeth, which perhaps explains why Elizabeth treated Mary with as much respect as possible, whereas Mary was often bullish in her dealings with Elizabeth. It is tempting to side with one monarch or the other, but the fact is that both Elizabeth and Mary were victims of circumstance, who were used as political and religious pawns in the long-standing power struggle between England and Scotland, Catholic and Protestant. One was bound to distrust, and ultimately dispatch, the other, and, in 1587, that is what happened.

MEETING QUEEN ELIZABETH I

She is a haughty woman, falling easily into rebuke…

WITNESSED BY
ANDRÉ HURAULT
AND PAUL HENTZNER

Elizabeth I, queen of England, from 1558 until her death in 1603, was a charismatic and formidable figure, not just in England but in Europe too. She had a reputation among foreign dignitaries for being 'majestical' in manner. When the French ambassador met her in 1597, she had been in power for forty years and was near the end of her reign.

THE WITNESSES

1) André Hurault, Sieur de Maisse, was Ambassador Extraordinary from King Heny IV of France to Queen Elizabeth. He landed in England on 30 November 1597 with the specific mission of finding out whether the queen was prepared to join in peace negotiations with Spain. While he was in England, Hurault saw Shakespeare's company act at Court. About this he only made the neutral comment, 'the sixth day they began to dance in the presence of the queen, and to act comedies which was done in the Great Chamber.'

He describes the elderly queen in all her power – and her quirkiness and vulnerability.

2) Paul Hentzner was the tutor of a young German nobleman whom he accompanied on a visit to England in 1598. These foreigners looked at the English queen with fresh, cold, unsentimental eyes, and instead of Gloriana they saw a wrinkled old woman.

THE WITNESSES' ACCOUNTS

1) André Hurault, Sieur de Maisse

I [de Maisse] reached London in the evening of the second day of the month of December, night having fallen, and was lodged in a house that the Queen had commanded for me wherein Drake had formerly lodged.

What I learned of the Queen and of the principal of her Council before I had seen either her of any of them is that when a man speaks to her, and especially when he says something displeasing, she interrupts not seldom; and by reason of her interruptions very often misunderstands what is said to her and misreports it to her Council. Hence comes the custom of delivering to the Council in writing what has been said to her. She is a haughty woman, falling easily into rebuke...

In her own nature she is very avaricious and when some expense is necessary her Councillors must deceive her before embarking her on it little by little. She thinks highly of herself and has little regard for her servants and Council, being of opinion that she is far wiser than they; she mocks them and often cries out upon them. On their part, they, even the Earl of Leicester, have given her a high opinion of her wisdom and prudence. She thinks also this is due to her age, saying quite freely that she was intended for affairs of state, even from her cradle; she told me so herself. She is sixty years old, and since the seventh of November last, 1597, in the fortieth year of her reign.

8 December [when de Maisse had an audience with the Queen]. She was strangely attired in a dress of silver cloth, white and crimson, or silver 'gauze', as they call it. This dress had slashed sleeves lined with red taffeta, and was girt about with other little sleeves, that hung down to the ground, which she was for ever twisting and untwisting. She kept the front of her dress open, and one could see the whole of her bosom, and passing low, and often she would open the front of this robe with her hands as if she was too hot. The collar of the robe was very high, and the lining of the inner part all adorned with rubies and pearls, very many, but quite small. She also had a chain of rubies and pearls about her neck.

On her head she wore a garland of the same material and beneath it a great reddish-coloured wig, with a great number of spangles of gold and silver, and hanging down over her forehead some pearls, but of no great worth. On either side of her ears hung two great curls of hair, almost down to her shoulders and within the collar of her robe, spangled as the top of her head. Her bosom is somewhat wrinkled, as well as one can see for the collar that she wears round her neck, but lower down[1] her flesh is exceedingly white and delicate, so far as one could see.

As for her face, it is and appears to be very aged. It is long and thin, and her teeth are very yellow and unequal, compared with what they were formerly, so they say, and on the left side less [teeth] than the right. Many of them are missing, so that one cannot understand her easily when she speaks quickly. Her figure is fair and tall and graceful in whatever she does; so far as may be she keeps her dignity, yet humbly and graciously withal.

All the time she spoke she would often rise from her chair and appear to be very impatient with what I was saying. She would complain that the fire was hurting her eyes, though there was a great screen before it and she six or seven feet away; yet did she give orders to have it extinguished,

---

1 – It is hard to imagine what of the Queen's flesh lower down might have been visible.

making them bring water to pour on it. She told me she was well pleased to stand up, and that she used to speak thus with ambassadors who came to seek her, and used sometimes to tire them, of which they would occasionally complain. I begged her not to overtire herself in any way, and I rose when she did; and then she sat down again, and so did I.

2) Paul Hentzer

Next came the Queen, in the sixty-fifth year of her age, as we were told, very majestic; her face oblong, fair, but wrinkled; her eyes small, yet black and pleasant; her nose a little hooked; her lips narrow; and her teeth black (a defect the English seem subject to, from their too great use of sugar); she had in her ears two pearls, with very rich drops; she wore false hair, and that red… her hands were small, her fingers long, and her stature neither tall nor low; her air was stately, her manner of speaking mild and obliging.

THE GUNPOWDER PLOT

Catesby propounded to have it performed by gunpowder, and by making a mine under the upper House of Parliament

WITNESSED BY
GUIDO (GUY) FAWKES

The Gunpowder Plot was a conspiracy to advance the Catholic cause in England. Its thrust was drastic in the extreme - to fill with gunpowder a cellar directly under the floor of the Upper House of Parliament, and ignite it when all the Lords, King James I and the Prince of Wales, Prince Henry, were assembled immediately above for the opening of Parliament in November 1605. In the past historians doubted whether the plot could have worked, but recent experiments have shown that the force of the explosion, contained and directed upwards by the stoutly built walls, would have killed everyone in the chamber. If successful, the Plot would have destroyed the entire English and Scottish establishment.

Questions still remain about the way the authorities got to hear about the plot and took action at the very last moment. The discovery of Guy Fawkes in the cellar, one of the most dramatic set-pieces of English history, may have been stage-managed by the authorities for maximum effect – to discredit the Catholics completely.

When arrested, Fawkes was taken directly to the king, who at one in the morning was in his bedchamber. There was a confrontation. Fawkes looked at the Scottish courtiers surrounding the king and boldly said he wanted to blow the Scots back into Scotland. Fawkes was tortured for several days under the supervision of Sir William Wade, Lieutenant of the Tower of London. The king gave specific instructions: 'The gentler tortures are to be first used and so by stages to the greatest, and so God speed your good work.' This produced the confession. Fawkes was sentenced to death by hanging, drawing and quartering, but he managed to escape this appalling fate by jumping off the scaffold and breaking his own neck.

THE WITNESS

Guido (Guy) Fawkes, born in York in 1570, was a soldier with a knowledge of gunpowder. He was one of half-a-dozen Catholic conspirators who were active in the plot to blow up James I. Fawkes was in the cellars when there was a security check ordered by the Secretary of State, and he was caught red-handed, while he was guarding the gunpowder. His confession was written only after torture.

THE WITNESS'S ACCOUNT

I confess, that a practice in general was first broken unto me, against his Majesty for the relief of the Catholic cause, and not invented or propounded by myself. And this was first propounded unto me about Easter last was twelve month beyond the seas, in the low countries of the Archduke's obeisance[1], by Thomas Winter, who came thereupon with me into England, and there we imparted our purpose to three other gentlemen more, namely, Robert Catesby, Thomas Percy and John Wright, who all five consulting together of the means how to execute the same, and taking a vow of ourselves for secrecy, Catesby

1 – Meaning the (Catholic-controlled) Spanish Netherlands.

propounded to have it performed by gunpowder, and by making a mine under the upper House of Parliament: which place we made a choice of the rather because religion having been unjustly suppressed there, it was fittest that justice and punishment should be executed there.

This being resolved amongst us, Thomas Percy hired an house at Westminster for that purpose, near adjoining to the Parliament House, and there we begun to make our mine about the 2 of December 1604.

The five that first entered into the work were Thomas Percy, Thomas Catesby, Thomas Winter, John Wright and myself: and soon after we took another unto us, Christopher Wright having sworn him also, and taken the Sacrament for secrecy.

When we came to the very foundation of the wall of the house, which was about three yards thick, and found it a matter of great difficulty, we took unto us another gentleman, Robert Winter, in like manner with oath and sacrament as afore said.

It was about Christmas when we brought our mine unto the wall, and about Candlemas [early February] we had wrought the wall halfway through; and whilst they were in working, I stood as sentinel to descry any man that came near, whereof I gave them warning, and so they ceased until I gave notice again to proceed.

All we seven lay in the house, and had shot and powder, being resolved to die in that place before we should yield or be taken. As they were working upon the wall they heard a rushing in the cellar of removing of coals, whereupon we feared we had been discovered. They sent me to go to the cellar, who finding that the coals were a-selling and that the cellar was to be let, viewing the commodity thereof for our purpose, Percy went and hired the same for yearly rent.

We had before this provided and brought into the house twenty barrels of powder, which we removed into the cellar, and covered the same with billets and faggots, which were provided for that purpose.

About Easter, the parliament being prorogued till October next, we dispersed ourselves and I retired into the low countries by advice and direction of the rest, as well to acquaint Owen[2] with the particulars of the plot, as also lest by my longer stay I might have grown suspicious[3] and so have come in question.

In the meantime Percy having the key of the cellar, laid in more powder and wood into it. I returned about the beginning of September next, and then receiving the key again of Percy, we brought in more powder and billets to cover the same again and so I went for a time into the country till the 30 of October.

It was a further resolve amongst us that the same day that this act should have been performed, some other of our confederates should have surprised the person of Lady Elizabeth the king's eldest daughter[4] who was kept in Warwickshire

2 – Hugh Owen, in the pay of the Spanish Netherlands.
3 – Aroused suspicion.
4 – Princess Elizabeth later became Elizabeth of Bohemia, 'the Winter Queen'.

153

at Lord Harrington's house, and presently have her proclaimed as queen, having a project of a proclamation ready for that purpose, wherein we made no mention of altering of religion, nor would have avowed the deed to be ours, until we should have power enough to make our party good and then we would have avowed both.

Concerning Duke Charles, the king's second son[5] we had sundry consultations how to seize on his person. But because we found no means how to compass it (the Duke being kept near London, where we had not forces enough) we resolved to serve our turn with the Lady Elizabeth.

5 – Prince Charles later succeeded his father as King Charles I.

THE GREAT FIRE OF LONDON

It made me weep to see it. The churches, houses, all on fire and flaming at once, and a horrid noise the flames made...

WITNESSED BY
SAMUEL PEPYS

The fire began in the night on 2 September 1666 as a small domestic fire at the bakehouse of Thomas Farynor in Pudding Lane. Because the shops and houses were densely packed, built of timber and roofed with thatch, the flames spread rapidly. As much as 80 per cent of the City of London was destroyed, including 89 churches and 13,000 other buildings; 100,000 people were left homeless.

THE WITNESS

Samuel Pepys (1633-1703) became a clerk in the English Exchequer in 1659. It was then that he started writing his famous Diary, which he had to give up after ten years because of failing eyesight. At the time of the Great Fire he was Clerk of the Acts of the Navy, a major administrative post at which he worked very hard. His conscientiousness, his eye for detail, his sympathy and concern for ordinary people in distress, his practicality – all show in his account of the fire.

THE WITNESS'S ACCOUNT

2 September. Lords Day. Some of our maids sitting up late last night to get things ready against our feast today, Jane called us up about three in the morning, to tell us of a great fire they saw in the City. So I rose and slipped on my nightgown and went to her window, and thought it to be on the backside of Marke-lane[1] at the farthest; but being unused to such fires as followed I thought it far enough off; and so went to bed again and to sleep. About seven rose again to dress myself, and there looked out at the window and saw the fire not so much as it was and further off. So to my closet to set things to rights after yesterday's cleaning. By and by Jane comes and tells me that she hears that above 300 houses have been burned down tonight by the fire we saw, and that it is now burning down all Fish-street by London Bridge.

So I made myself ready presently and walked to the Tower, and there got up upon one of the high

1 – It was common at that time to write street names in this way. So what we would now write as Marke Lane was then written Marke-lane.

places, Sir J. Robinson's little son going up with me; and there I did see the houses[2] at that end of the bridge all on fire, and an infinite great fire on this and the other side the end of the bridge; which, among other people, did trouble me for poor little Michell and our Sarah on the bridge. So down, with my heart full of trouble, to the Lieutenant of the Tower, who tells me that it begun this morning in the King's baker's house in Pudding-lane, and that it hath burned St. Magnus's Church and most part of Fish-street already. So I down to the water-side, and there got a boat and through bridge, and there saw a lamentable fire. Poor Michell's house, as far as the Old Swan, already burned that way, and the fire running further, that in a very little time it got as far as the Steeleyard[3] while I was there. Everybody endeavouring to remove their goods and flinging into the river or bringing them into lighters that lay off; poor people staying in their houses as long as till the very fire touched them, and then running into boats, or clambering from

2 – Old London Bridge had houses built along both sides.
3 – The walled London trading centre of the Hanseatic League, on the site of Cannon Street Station.

one pair of stairs by the water-side to another. And among other things, the poor pigeons, I perceive, were loath to leave their houses, but hovered about the windows and balconies till they were, some of them burned, their wings, and fell down.

....

"it begun this morning in the King's baker's house in Pudding-lane"

....

Having stayed, and in an hour's time seen the fire rage every way, and nobody to my sight endeavouring to quench it, but to remove their goods and leave all to the fire; and having seen it get as far as the Steelyard, and the wind mighty high and driving it into the City; and everything, after so long a drought, proving combustible, even the very stones of churches. I to Whitehall with a gentleman who desired to go off from the Tower to see the fire in my boat; to Whitehall, and there up to the Kings closet in the chapel, where people came about me and I did give them an account dismayed them all, and word was carried in to the King.

So I was called for, and did tell the King and Duke of York[4] what I saw, and that unless his Majesty did command houses to be pulled down[5] nothing could stop the fire. They seemed much troubled, and the King commanded me to go to my Lord Mayor from him, and command him to spare no houses, but to pull down before the fire every way. The Duke of York bid me tell him that if he would have any more soldiers he shall. Here meeting with Captain Cocke, I in his coach, which he lent me, and Creed with me, to Paul's, and there walked along Watling-street as well as I could, every creature coming away loaden with goods to save, and here and there sick people carried away in beds. Extraordinary good goods carried in carts and on backs.

4 – Charles II's brother, who would succeed Charles as
James II.
5 – To make a fire-break.

At last met my Lord Mayor [Sir Thomas Bloodworth] in Canning-street, like a man spent, with a handkercher about his neck. To the King's message he cried like a fainting woman, 'Lord! what can I do? I am spent! People will not obey me. I have been pulling down houses; but the fire overtakes us faster than we can do it.' That for himself he must go and refresh himself, having been up all night. So he left me and I him, and walked home – seeing people all almost distracted and no manner of means to quench the fire. The houses too, so very thick hereabouts and full of matter for burning, as pitch and tar – and warehouses of oil and wines and brandy. . .

Met with the King and Duke of York in their barge and [went] with them to Queen Hithe and there called Sir Rd. Browne to them. Their order was to pull down houses apace; but little was done, the fire coming upon them so fast. Having seen as much as I could now, I away to Whitehall by appointment, and there walked to James's Park and there met my wife and Creed and Wood and his wife, and walked to my boat; and there upon the water again and to the fire, it still increasing, and the wind great.

When we could endure no more upon the water, we to a little ale-house, and there stayed till it was almost dark and saw the fire grow; and as it grew darker, appeared more and more, as far as we could see up the hill of the City, in a most horrid malicious bloody flame. We saw the fire as only one entire arch of fire above a mile long. It made me weep to see it. The churches, houses, all on fire and flaming at once, and a horrid noise the flames made, and the cracking of houses at their ruin. So home with a sad heart.

THE BOSTON TEA PARTY

Let every man do his duty, and be true to his country

WITNESSED BY
GEORGE ROBERT TWELVES HEWES

The expectation that the American colonies would pay for their defence was reasonable, but the British government was inept in the way that it imposed its taxes. When the colonists claimed they should not have to pay taxation without representation, the government retracted all but the tax on tea. The arrival of three tea ships, the *Dartmouth*, the *Eleanor* and the *Beaver*, in Boston harbour triggered a strong reaction. On 16 December 1773, 7,000 Bostonians gathered on the wharf and decided that the tea ships must leave without any duty being paid. This message was conveyed to the collector of customs, but he refused to let the ships leave until the duty was paid. Then 200 Bostonians disguised as Indians boarded the three ships and threw 342 crates of tea into the harbour.

THE WITNESS

George Robert Twelves Hewes was a Boston shoemaker who took part in several of the key events of the American Revolution. It was not until fifty years later that he told James Hawkes about his involvement in the Boston Massacre and the Boston Tea Party. Hawkes published Hewes' reminiscence in 1834.

Hewes wore his Indian disguise to ensure his anonymity among his fellow Bostonians.

THE WITNESS'S ACCOUNT

The tea destroyed was contained in three ships, lying near each other at what was called at that time Griffin's wharf, and were surrounded by armed ships of war, the commanders of which had publicly declared that if the rebels, as they were pleased to style the Bostonians, should not withdraw their opposition to the landing of the tea before a certain day, the 17th day of December, 1773, they should on that day force it on shore, under the cover of their cannon's mouth.

On the day preceding the seventeenth, there was

a meeting of the citizens of the county of Suffolk, convened at one of the churches in Boston, for the purpose of consulting on what measures might be considered expedient to prevent the landing of the tea, or secure the people from the collection of the duty. At that meeting a committee was appointed to wait on Governor Hutchinson, and request him to inform them whether he would take any measures to satisfy the people on the object of the meeting.

To the first application of this committee, the Governor told them he would give them a definite answer by five o'clock in the afternoon. At the hour appointed, the committee again repaired to the Governor's house, and on inquiry found he had gone to his country seat at Milton, a distance of about six miles. When the committee returned and informed the meeting of the absence of the Governor, there was a confused murmur among the members, and the meeting was immediately dissolved, many of them crying out, 'Let every man do his duty, and be true to his country'; and there was a general huzza[1] for Griffin's wharf.

It was now evening, and I immediately dressed myself in the costume of an Indian, equipped with a small hatchet, which I and my associates denominated the tomahawk, with which, and a club, after having painted my face and hands with coal dust in the shop of a blacksmith, I repaired to Griffin's wharf, where the ships lay that contained the tea. When I first appeared in the street after being thus disguised, I fell in with many who were dressed, equipped and painted as I was, and who fell in with me and marched in order to the place of our destination.

When we arrived at the wharf, there were three of our number who assumed an authority to direct our operations, to which we readily submitted. They divided us into three parties, for the purpose of boarding the three ships which contained the tea at the same time. The name of him who commanded the division to which I was assigned was Leonard Pitt. The names of the other

1 – A sailor's cheer, pronounced 'her-zah', similar to 'hurrah'.

commanders I never knew. We were immediately ordered by the respective commanders to board all the ships at the same time, which we promptly obeyed.

The commander of the division to which I belonged, as soon as we were on board the ship, appointed me boatswain, and ordered me to go to the captain and demand of him the keys to the hatches and a dozen candles. I made the demand accordingly, and the captain promptly delivered the articles, but requested me to do no damage to the ship. We then were ordered by our commander to open the hatches and take out all the chests of tea and throw them overboard, and we immediately proceeded to execute his orders, first cutting and splitting the chests with our tomahawks, so as thoroughly to expose them to the effects of the water.

In about three hours from the time we went on board, we had thus broken and thrown overboard every tea chest to be found in the ship, while those in the other ships were disposing of the tea in the same way. We were surrounded by British armed ships, but no attempt was made to resist us.

We then quietly retired to our several places of residence, without having any conversation with each other, or taking any measures to discover who were our associates; nor do I recollect of our having had the knowledge of the name of a single individual concerned in that affair, except that of Leonard Pitt, the commander of my division, whom I have mentioned. There appeared to be an understanding that each individual should volunteer his services, keep his own secret, and risk the consequence for himself. No disorder took place during that transaction, and it was observed at that time that the stillest night ensued that Boston had enjoyed for many months.

....

"we immediately proceeded to execute his orders, first cutting and splitting the chests with our tomahawks, so as thoroughly to expose them to the effects of the water"

....

During the time we were throwing the tea overboard, there were several attempts made by some of the citizens of Boston and its vicinity to carry off small quantities of it for their family use. They would watch their opportunity to snatch up a handful from the deck and put it into their pockets.

One Captain O'Connor, whom I well knew, came on board for that purpose, and when he supposed he was not noticed, filled his pockets, and also the lining of his coat. But I had detected him and gave information to the captain of what he was doing. We were ordered to take him into custody, and just as he was stepping from the vessel, I seized him by the skirt of his coat, and in attempting to pull him back, I tore it off; but, springing forward, by a rapid effort he made his escape. He had, however, to run a gauntlet through the crowd upon the wharf nine each one, as he passed, giving him a kick or a stroke.

The next morning, after we had cleared the ships of the tea, it was discovered that considerable quantities of it were floating upon the surface of the water; and to prevent the possibility of any of its being saved for use, a number of small boats were manned by sailors and citizens, who rowed them into those parts of the harbour wherever the tea was visible, and by beating it with oars and paddles so thoroughly drenched it as to render its entire destruction inevitable.

THE DEATH OF NELSON

The ball struck the epaulette on his left shoulder, and penetrated his chest. He fell with his face on the deck

WITNESSED BY
DOCTOR WILLIAM BEATTY, MD

The Battle of Trafalgar, one of the greatest sea battles in British history, was fought off the coast of Portugal on 21 October 1805. The British Fleet, commanded by Horatio, Lord Nelson, defeated a combined French and Spanish fleet. The fighting was at very close quarters and Nelson's flagship, *HMS Victory*, became entangled with the French ship *Redoubtable*. A French sniper perched high in the rigging of the *Redoubtable* fired down at Nelson, who was an unmissable target in his dress uniform and wearing all his honours.

Nelson was carried below decks, mortally wounded but living long enough to hear the news of his fleet's victory.

THE WITNESS

Dr William Beatty, MD, was the naval surgeon aboard *HMS Victory* who attended Nelson as he lay dying. The doctor published his detailed account soon after the battle. This is an extract from it.

The Battle of Trafalgar

Nelson's famous victory at the Battle of Trafalgar represented the defeat of Napoleon's plans to invade England, and helped to secure Britain's position as the most powerful naval force in the world, a reputation that would underpin the success of the British empire and last for over 100 years. The Battle of Trafalgar took place on the 21 October 1805 at Cape Trafalgar, off the western coast of Spain. It involved the French and Spanish fleets, under the command of Admiral Villeneuve, and the British Navy under the command of Admiral Nelson. The British were heavily outnumbered. In addition, many of the Spanish ships carried more guns than those of the British. However, the British were particularly well-drilled and could fire their guns at least twice for every French and Spanish shot.

In battle much of the action happened at

very close range, ships firing at one another from only a few metres away. The guns fired heavy cannon balls and chain and link shot designed to wreck rigging, but they could also cause enormous injury to a human being, ripping off limbs and sending lethal splinters flying in all directions – it is said that some of the French troops were so terrified of enemy fire that they closed their gun ports, in an attempt to avoid the onslaught.

THE WITNESS SETS THE SCENE

Lord Nelson and Captain Hardy walked the quarter-deck in conversation for some time, while the enemy kept up an incessant raking fire. A double-headed shot struck one of the parties of Marines drawn up on the poop, and killed eight of them; when his lordship, perceiving this, ordered Captain Adair to disperse his men round the ship, that they might not suffer so much from being together. In a few minutes afterwards a shot struck the fore-brace-bits on the quarter-deck, and passed between Lord Nelson and Captain Hardy; a splinter from the bits bruising Captain Hardy's foot, and tearing the buckle from his shoe. They both instantly stopped; and were observed by the officers on deck to survey each other with inquiring looks, each supposing the other to be wounded. His lordship then smiled, and said: 'This is too warm work, Hardy, to last long.'

Character Profiles

Horatio, Lord Nelson

Horatio, Lord Nelson was born the son of a clergyman in Burnham Thorpe, Norfolk, England, in 1758, the sixth of eleven children. He joined the navy at the age of 12 and went to serve on a ship captained by a maternal uncle. At 20 years old Nelson became a captain, and saw service in the West Indies, Canada and the Baltic. When Britain entered the French revolutionary wars, Nelson was put in charge of his favourite ship, the *Agamemnon*. He served in the Mediterranean, helped to capture Corsica and took part in the battle at Calvi, during which he lost the use of his right eye. Later, in 1797, he lost his right arm during the Battle of Santa Cruz de Tenerife. As a military commander, Nelson was hailed as a national hero even before his death at the Battle of Trafalgar – the only British military commander who could rival Napoleon Bonaparte in strategic expertise. Indeed, Napoleon himself kept a bust of Nelson in his own private quarters. Nelson was known as something of a maverick. He was highly respected, even loved, by his men, but he occasionally ignored the orders of his superior officers, opting for tactics that were eccentric and reckless. His wayward attitude, charismatic personality, deep sense of honour and fierce patriotism made Nelson one of the most popular figures in British history.

Sir Thomas Hardy

Thomas Masterman Hardy was captain under Nelson on board *HMS Victory* at the Battle of Trafalgar. He was born in Dorset to Joseph and Nanny Hardy in 1769, and, like Nelson, joined the navy at the age of 12. From the beginning of his naval career Hardy found he was popular with his superiors and messmates alike, and he progressed quickly through the naval ranks. Hardy often attributed the success of his relationship with Lord Nelson to the fact that he always knew his place and respected Nelson's authority. He is known to have said that it lay in 'my being First Lieutenant when you like to be Captain, and Flag Captain when you take a fancy to being Admiral'.

THE WITNESS'S ACCOUNT

About fifteen minutes past one o'clock, which was in the heat of the engagement, he was walking the middle of the quarter-deck with Captain Hardy, and in the act of turning near the hatchway with his face towards the stern of the *Victory*, when the fatal ball was fired from the enemy's mizzen-top.

The ball struck the epaulette on his left shoulder, and penetrated his chest. He fell with his face on the deck. Captain Hardy, who was on his right (the side furthest from the enemy) and advanced some steps before his lordship, on turning round, saw the Sergeant Major of Marines with two seamen raising him from the deck; where he had fallen on the same spot on which, a little before, his secretary had breathed his last, with whose blood his lordship's clothes were much soiled. Captain Hardy expressed a hope that he was not severely wounded; to which the gallant Chief replied: 'They have done for me at last, Hardy.' – 'I hope not,' answered Captain Hardy. 'Yes,' replied his lordship; 'my backbone is shot through.'

Captain Hardy ordered the seamen to carry the Admiral to the cockpit. His lordship was laid upon a bed, stripped of his clothes, and covered with a sheet. [Nelson] said to Doctor Scott, 'Doctor, I told you so. Doctor, I am gone,' and after a short pause he added in a low voice, 'I have to leave Lady Hamilton, and my adopted daughter Horatia, as a legacy to my country.' The surgeon then examined the wound, assuring his lordship that he would not put him to much pain in endeavouring to discover the course of the ball; which he soon found had penetrated deep into the chest, and had probably lodged in the spine. This being explained to his lordship, he replied, he was confident his back was shot through.

The back was then examined externally, but without any injury being perceived; on which his lordship was requested by the surgeon to make him acquainted with all his sensations. He replied, that he felt a gush of blood every minute within his breast: that he had no feeling in the lower part of his body: and that his breathing was difficult, and attended with very severe pain about that part of the spine where he was confident that the ball had struck; 'for,' said he, 'I felt it break my back.' These symptoms, but more particularly the gush of blood which his lordship complained of, together with the state of his pulse, indicated to the surgeon the hopeless situation of the case; but till after the victory was ascertained and announced to his lordship, the true nature of his wound was concealed by the surgeon from all on board except only Captain Hardy, Doctor Scott, Mr Burke, and Messrs Smith and Westemburg the assistant surgeons.

The *Victory*'s crew cheered whenever they observed an enemy's ship surrender. He now felt an ardent thirst; and frequently called for drink, and to be fanned with paper, making use of these words: 'Fan, fan,' and 'Drink, drink.' Lemonade, and wine and water were given to him occasionally.

An hour and ten minutes elapsed, from the time of his lordship's being wounded, before Captain Hardy's first subsequent interview with him. They shook hands affectionately, and Lord Nelson said: 'Well, Hardy, how goes the battle? How goes the day with us?' – 'Very well, my Lord,' replied Captain Hardy. 'I am a dead man, Hardy. I am going fast: it will be all over with me soon. Come nearer to me. Pray let my dear Lady Hamilton have my hair, and all other things belonging to me.' Captain Hardy observed, that he hoped Mr Beatty could yet hold out some prospect of life. – 'Oh! no,' answered his lordship; 'it is impossible. My back is shot through. Beatty will tell you so.' Captain Hardy then returned on deck, and at parting shook hands again with his revered friend and commander.

....

"Don't throw me overboard, Hardy"

....

Captain Hardy came to see his Lordship a second time after about fifty minutes. He congratulated him on his brilliant victory. His Lordship answered, '*Anchor*, Hardy, *anchor*!' He then told Captain Hardy he felt that in a few minutes he should be no more, adding in a low tone, 'Don't throw me overboard, Hardy.' The Captain answered: 'Oh! no, certainly not.' 'Then,' replied his Lordship, 'You know what to do: and take care of my dear Lady Hamilton, Hardy. Kiss me, Hardy.' The Captain now knelt down and kissed his cheek; when his Lordship said, 'Now I am satisfied. Thank God I have done my duty.' Captain Hardy stood for a minute or two in silent contemplation: then he knelt down again, and kissed his Lordship's forehead.

He called for 'drink, drink,' 'fan, fan,' and 'rub, rub,' addressing in the last case Dr Scott, who had been rubbing his Lordship's breast with his hand, from which he found some relief. These words he spoke in a very rapid manner, which rendered articulation difficult: but he every now and then made a greater effort with his vocal powers, and pronounced distinctly these last words: 'Thank God, I have done my duty.'

THE BATTLE OF WATERLOO

One might suppose that nothing could have resisted the shock of this terrible moving mass

WITNESSED BY
CAPTAIN J. H. GRONOW

The Battle of Waterloo was the key event in 19th century European history. The Allies massed their forces for a final showdown with the French Emperor. A British force of 68,000 under the Duke of Wellington encamped in Belgium, as did a massive Prussian army of 89,000 led by Field Marshal Blücher. Napoleon advanced his army of 105,000 troops into Belgium in the hope of outnumbering and defeating the British and Prussian armies separately, rather than facing them together. The French succeeded in routing the Prussians at Ligny on 16 June 1815, then turned to deal with the British at Waterloo, a few miles south of Brussels on 18 June. Napoleon might well have defeated Wellington, but for the timely arrival of Blücher during the battle. Napoleon's defeat at the Battle of Waterloo meant that he had to abdicate.

THE WITNESS

Captain J. H. Gronow was a British officer. He joined the British Army at 19 and served under Wellington in both Spain and Belgium.

THE WITNESS'S ACCOUNT

On the morning of the 18th the sun shone most gloriously, and so clear was the atmosphere that we could see the long, imposing lines of the enemy most distinctly.

The whole of the British infantry not actually engaged were at that time formed into squares; and as you looked along our lines, it seemed as if we formed a continuous wall of human beings. I recollect distinctly being able to see Bonaparte and his staff; and some of my brother officers using the glass, exclaimed, 'There he is on his white horse.'

I should not forget to state that when the enemy's artillery began to play on us, we had orders to lie down, when we could hear the shot and shell whistling around us, killing and wounding great numbers; then again we were ordered on our knees to receive cavalry. The French artillery - which consisted of three hundred guns, though we did not muster more than half that number - committed terrible havoc during the early part of the battle, whilst we were acting on the defensive.

About 4 pm the enemy's artillery in front of us ceased firing all of a sudden, and we saw large masses of cavalry advance: not a man present who survived could have forgotten in after life the awful grandeur of that charge. You discovered at a distance what appeared to be an overwhelming, long moving line, which, ever advancing, glittered like a stormy wave of the sea when it catches the sunlight. On they came until they got near enough, whilst the very earth seemed to vibrate beneath the thundering tramp of the mounted host. One might suppose that nothing could have resisted the shock of this terrible moving mass.

They were the famous cuirassiers, almost all old soldiers, who had distinguished themselves on most of the battlefields of Europe. In an almost incredibly short period they were within twenty yards of us, shouting 'Vive l'Empéreur!' The word of command, 'Prepare to receive cavalry,' had been given, every man in the front ranks knelt, and a wall bristling with steel, held together by steady hands, presented itself to the infuriated cuirassiers.

I should observe that just before this charge the duke [of Wellington] entered by one of the angles of the square, accompanied only by one aide-de-camp; all the rest of his staff being either killed or wounded. Our commander-in-chief, as far as I could judge, appeared perfectly composed; but looked very thoughtful and pale.

"We had now before us probably about 20,000 of the best soldiers in France"

The charge of the French cavalry was gallantly executed; but our well-directed fire brought men and horses down, and ere long the utmost confusion arose in their ranks. The officers were exceedingly brave, and by their gestures and fearless bearing did all in their power to encourage their men to form again and renew the attack. The duke sat unmoved, mounted on his favourite charger. I recollect his asking the Hon. Lieut.-Colonel Stanhope what o'clock it was, upon which Stanhope took out his watch, and said it was twenty minutes past four. The Duke replied, 'The battle is mine; and if the Prussians arrive soon, there will be an end of the war.'

It was about five o'clock on that memorable day,

that we suddenly received orders to retire behind an elevation in our rear. The enemy's artillery had come up en masse within a hundred yards of us. By the time they began to discharge their guns, we were lying down behind the rising ground, and protected by the ridge.

Up came the whole mass of the Imperial infantry of the Guard, led on by the Emperor in person. We had now before us probably about 20,000 of the best soldiers in France, the heroes of many memorable victories; we saw the bearskin caps rising higher and higher as they ascended the ridge of ground which separated us, and advanced nearer and nearer to our lines.

It was at this moment the Duke of Wellington gave his famous order for our bayonet charge, as he rode along the line: these are the precise words he made use of – 'Guards, get up and charge!' We were instantly on our legs, and after so many hours of inaction and irritation at maintaining a purely defensive attitude - all the time suffering the loss of comrades and friends - the spirit which animated officers and men may easily be imagined. After firing a volley as soon as the enemy were within shot, we rushed on with fixed bayonets, and that hearty hurrah peculiar to British soldiers.

Early on the morning after the battle of Waterloo, I visited Huguemont, in order to witness with my own eyes the traces of one of the most hotly-contested spots of the field of battle. I came first upon the orchard, and there discovered heaps of dead men, in various uniforms: those of the Guards in their usual red jackets, the German Legion in green, and the French dressed in blue, mingled together. The dead and the wounded positively covered the whole area of the orchard; not less than two thousand men had there fallen… On this spot I lost some of my dearest and bravest friends, and the country had to mourn many of its most heroic sons slain here.

According to the custom of commanding officers, whose business it is after a great battle to report to the Commander-in-Chief, the muster-roll of fame always closes before the rank of captain[1]. It has always appeared to me a great injustice that there should ever be any limit to the roll of gallantry. If a captain, lieutenant, an ensign, a sergeant or a private has distinguished himself, their deeds ought to be reported, in order that the sovereign and nation should know who really fight the great battles of England. There were many of even superior rank who were omitted to be mentioned in the public despatches.

Thus, for example, to the individual courage of Lord Saltoun and Charley Ellis, who commanded the light companies, was mainly owing our success at Huguemont. The same may be said of Needham, Percival, Erskine, Grant, Vyner, Buckley, Master, and young Algernon Greville, who at that time could not have been more than seventeen years old.

1 – No-one of the rank of captain or below was mentioned by name.

NAPOLEON GOES INTO EXILE

Complaints from me would be beneath my dignity and character; I must either command or be silent

WITNESSED BY
COMTE DE LAS CASES
AND SIR HUDSON LOWE

After Napoleon's final defeat at the Battle of
Waterloo in June 1815, the European powers
would take no further chances with him. They
exiled him to the extremely isolated island of St
Helena in the South Atlantic Ocean.

THE WITNESSES

1) Among the small entourage that accompanied
the deposed emperor into exile was Emmanuel,
Comte de Las Cases (1766-1842). Napoleon
dictated part of his memoirs to de Las Cases,
whose famous *Memorial* was published in
1823. This was hailed as a bible by Napoleon
worshippers, but is regarded by historians as not
entirely reliable.

2) Sir Hudson Lowe (1769-1844) was an Anglo-
English military commander who was present
at 13 major battles in the Napoleonic Wars.
From 1816 he was Governor of St Helena and
therefore Napoleon's 'gaoler'. There was friction
because Lowe was unwilling to be flexible about

the amount of freedom he would allow Napoleon; Napoleon's servants thought him unreasonable. After Napoleon's death, the British establishment showed Lowe little gratitude, apart from an eventual knighthood. Wellington said he had been 'a very bad choice; he was a man wanting in education and judgement. He was a stupid man.' The account is Lowe's own record of his conversation with Napoleon at their first meeting; he wrote it down in a mixture of English, Italian and French.

THE WITNESSES' ACCOUNTS

1) Comte de Las Cases

August 10, 1815 This day we cleared the Channel. We had now entered upon the dreary unknown course to which fate had doomed us. Again my agonies were renewed; again the dear connections I had abandoned resumed their sway over my heart. . . Meanwhile we advanced in our course and were soon to be out of Europe. Thus, in less than six weeks, had the emperor abdicated his throne and placed himself in the hands of the English, who were now hurrying him to a barren rock in the midst of a vast ocean. This is certainly no ordinary instance of the chances of fortune, and no common trial of firmness of mind.

October 23-24 The Emperor Napoleon, who lately possessed such boundless power and disposed of so many crowns, now occupies a wretched hovel a few feet square, which is perched upon a rock, unprovided with furniture, and without either shutters or curtains to the windows. This place must serve him for bedchamber, dressing room, dining room, study and sitting room; and he is obliged to go out when it is necessary to have this one apartment cleaned. His meals, consisting of a few wretched dishes, are brought to him from a distance, as though he were a criminal in a dungeon. He is absolutely in want of the necessaries of life: the bread and wine are not only not such as he has been accustomed to, but are so bad that we loathe to touch them; water, coffee, butter, oil and other articles are either not to be procured or are scarcely fit for use. . .

We were all assembled around the emperor, and he was recapitulating these facts with warmth[1]: 'For what infamous treatment are we reserved!' he exclaimed. 'This is the anguish of death. To injustice and violence they now add insult and protracted torment. If I were so hateful to them, why did they not get rid of me? A few musket balls in my heart or my head would have done the business, and there would at least have been some energy in the crime. Were it not for you, and above all for your wives, I would receive nothing from them but the pay of a private soldier. How can the monarchs of Europe permit the sacred character of sovereignty to be violated in my person? Do they not see that they are, with their own hands, working their own destruction at St Helena?'

'I entered their capitals victorious and, had I cherished such sentiments, what would have

1 – Emotion, passion or anger.

become of them? They styled me their brother, and I had become so by the choice of the people, the sanction of victory, the character of religion, and the alliances of their policy and their blood. Do they imagine that the good sense of nations is blind to their conduct? And what do they expect from it? At all events, make your complaints, gentlemen; let indignant Europe hear them. Complaints from me would be beneath my dignity and character; I must either command or be silent.'

2) Sir Hudson Lowe

17 April 1816 Had my first interview with him at four o'clock in the afternoon – was accompanied to his house by Rear Admiral Sir George Cockburn – General Bertrand received us in his dining room, serving as an antechamber and instantly afterwards ushered me into an inner room, where I found him (General Bonaparte) standing, having his hat in his hand – not addressing me when I came in but apparently waiting for me to speak, I broke the silence…

'We will speak then in Italian,' he said, and immediately commenced in that language a conversation, which lasted about half an hour, the purport of which was principally as follows. He first asked me where I had served – how I liked the Corsicans. He asked me if I had not been in Egypt with them, and in my replying in the affirmative, entered into a long discussion respecting that Country. 'Menou was a weak man – if Kléber had been there you would have all been made prisoners.'[2] He then passed in review all our operations in that country, with which he seemed as well acquainted as if he had himself been there, blamed [Sir Ralph] Abercromby for not landing sooner…

The subject of Egypt was again resumed. It was the most important geographical point in the world, and had always been considered so. He

2 – When Napoleon returned to France, he left the very
capable General Jean-Baptiste Kléber to succeed in
command in Egypt. When Kléber was assassinated by
a Syrian student, he was succeeded by General Jacques
François Menou. Under Menou, the French were defeated by
Abercromby at the Battle of Aboukir in March 1801; Cairo
had to be surrendered in June; the last French troops left for
France in September.

had reconnoitred the line of the [proposed] canal across the Isthmus of Suez and had calculated the expense of it at 10 or 12 millions of Livres. That a powerful Colony being established there it would have been impossible for us to have preserved our empire in India. He fell again to rallying at Menou.

He then asked me some further questions regarding myself. Whether I was not married. If I had not become so shortly before my leaving England. How I liked St Helena. I replied I had not been a sufficient time here to form a judgment upon it. After a short pause he asked how many years I had been in the service –

'28,' I replied.

BOARDING A SLAVE SHIP

They were all branded like sheep with the owner's marks of different forms

WITNESSED BY
REVEREND ROBERT WALSH

The slave trade was formally abolished by Act of Parliament in Britain in 1807. This was followed within a few months by parallel legislation in the United States – a law banning the importing of slaves. These acts did nothing to prevent or limit the buying and selling of slaves within America, but it did bring to an end the open shipping of black slaves across the Atlantic from Africa to America.

British and American coastguards patrolled the seas off the coast of Africa, stopping suspected slave ships. When slaves were found on board, the ships were confiscated and the slaves were taken back to Africa. Conditions on board the slave ships were appalling. Men, women and children were crammed into every available space.

THE WITNESS

The Reverend Robert Walsh served on one of the ships assigned to intercept the slavers off the African coast. On 22 May, 1829, a suspected slaver was sighted and the naval vessel set off in pursuit. The following day, a favourable wind allowed the interceptor to gain on the slaver, getting close enough to fire two shots across her bow. The slaver hove to, allowing an armed party from the interceptor to scrambled aboard. The Reverend Robert Walsh was among the boarding party.

The Transatlantic Slave Trade

For 200 years Portugal dominated the export of slaves from west Africa. During the 450 years that the transatlantic slave trade operated, Portuguese slavers were responsible for transporting over 4.5 million African people into slavery, over 40 per cent of the final total. Britain was also heavily involved in slavery, and many major ports, such as Liverpool, London and Bristol, prospered largely due to this trade in human traffic. During the 18th century, Britain was responsible for the export of 2.5 million African people.

Expanding European empires of the New World lacked one vital resource – a strong and resilient work force. The indigenous American people could not be used for slavery, because many of them had been weakened by diseases brought to America by European settlers. The Europeans themselves were unused to the warm climate and were not able to work in the heat, they also suffered from tropical diseases. Africans were excellent workers, accustomed as they were to the heat and experienced in agriculture and the keeping of cattle. They were resistant to many of the diseases that were killing off the Europeans. In short, the settlers saw them as the perfect slave race. West Africans were favourable over slaves from Muslim dominated North Africa, because north Africans had a tendency to be better educated, and therefore more likley to rebel. As one can see from Robert Walsh's account of the *Feloz*, the conditions on the slaving ships were barbaric and cruel. Often the human cargo was treated worse than livestock. Many slaves died en route to their new lives, from dysentry and malnutrition which set in during the forced marches and internment they had to endure whilst still on land. This explains why many of the deaths occurred only two weeks into the voyage. Robert Walsh boarded the *Feloz* after it had been at sea for 17 days, by which time 55 people had died and been thrown over-board.

THE WITNESS SETS THE SCENE

The first object that struck us was an enormous gun, turning on a swivel, on deck - the constant appendage of a pirate; and the next were large kettles[1] for cooking, on the bows - the usual apparatus of a slaver. Our boat was now hoisted out, and I went on board with the officers. When

1 – Cauldrons.

we mounted her decks we found her full of slaves. She was called the *Feloz*, commanded by Captain José Barbosa, bound to Bahia[2]. She was a very broad-decked ship, with a mainmast, schooner rigged, and behind her foremast was that large, formidable gun, which turned on a broad circle of iron, on deck, and which enabled her to act as a pirate if her slaving speculation failed. She had taken in, on the coast of Africa, 336 males and 226 females, making in all 562, and had been out seventeen days, during which she had thrown overboard 55.[3]

Character Profile

Reverend Robert Walsh

Robert Walsh was born in Waterford, Ireland in 1772. He was ordained in 1802, and appointed as a curate in Dublin before moving to the curacy of Finglas in 1806. In 1820, he was sent to Constantinople to act as chaplain to the British Embassy, and he used this

2 – In north-east Brazil.
3 – The death rate on these voyages was always high.

opportunity to travel through Turkey and Asia, where, having obtained a medical degree, he practised as a physician. From Constantinople he moved to the British embassy in St Petersburg, Russia, where he remained for a little while before moving again, this time to the sunnier climes of Rio De Janerio, Brazil.

By this time Walsh was a well-travelled, and well-informed man, and he came to be thought of as something of an expert in the field of slavery, because he had visited so many countries and observed so many different slaving regimes. His observations following the boarding of the *Feloz* brings home the horrifying reality of the existence aboard one of these ships.

THE WITNESS'S ACCOUNT

The slaves were all enclosed under grated hatchways between decks. The space was so low that they sat between each other's legs and

[were] stowed so close together that there was no possibility of their lying down or at all changing their position by night or day. As they belonged to and were shipped on account of different individuals, they were all branded like sheep with the owner's marks of different forms. These were impressed under their breasts or on their arms, and, as the mate informed me with perfect indifference 'burnt with the red-hot iron.' Over the hatchway stood a ferocious-looking fellow with a scourge of many twisted thongs in his hand, who was the slave driver of the ship, and whenever he heard the slightest noise below, he shook it over them and seemed eager to exercise it. I was quite pleased to take this hateful badge out of his hand, and I have kept it ever since as a horrid memorial of reality, should I ever be disposed to forget the scene I witnessed.

As soon as the poor creatures saw us looking down at them, their dark and melancholy visages brightened up. They perceived something of sympathy and kindness in our looks which they had not been accustomed to, and, feeling instinctively that we were friends, they immediately began to shout and clap their hands. One or two had picked up a few Portuguese words, and cried out, *'Viva! Viva!'* The women were particularly excited. They all held up their arms, and when we bent down and shook hands with them, they could not contain their delight; they endeavoured to scramble up on their knees, stretching up to kiss our hands, and we understood that they knew we were come to liberate them. Some, however, hung down their heads in apparently hopeless dejection; some were greatly emaciated, and some, particularly children, seemed dying.

But the circumstance which struck us most forcibly was how it was possible for such a number of human beings to exist, packed up and wedged together as tight as they could cram, in low cells three feet high, the greater part of which, except that immediately under the grated hatchways, was shut out from light or air, and this when the thermometer, exposed to the open sky, was standing in the shade, on our deck, at 89 [degrees Fahrenheit]. The space between decks was divided into two compartments 3 feet 3 inches high; the size of one was 16 feet by 18 and of the other 40 by 21; into the first were crammed the women and girls, into the second the men and boys. We also found manacles and fetters of different kinds, but it appears that they had all been taken off before we boarded.

The heat of these horrid places was so great and the odour so offensive that it was quite impossible to enter them, even had there been room. They were measured as above when the slaves had left them. The officers insisted that the poor suffering creatures should be admitted on deck to get air and water. This was opposed by the mate of the slaver, who, from a feeling that they deserved it, declared they would murder them all. The officers, however, persisted, and the poor beings were all turned up together. It is impossible to conceive the effect of this eruption - 517 fellow creatures of all ages and sexes, some children, some adults, some old men and women, all in a state of total nudity, scrambling out together to taste the luxury of a little fresh air and water. They came swarming up like bees from the aperture of a hive till the whole deck was crowded to suffocation stem to stern, so that it was impossible to imagine where they could all have come from or how they could have been stowed away.

....

"many of the survivors were seen lying about the decks in the last stage of emaciation and in a state of filth and misery not to be looked at "

....

After enjoying for a short time the unusual luxury of air, some water was brought; it was then that the extent of their sufferings was exposed in a fearful manner. They all rushed like maniacs towards it. No entreaties or threats or blows could restrain them; they shrieked and struggled and fought with one another for a drop of this precious liquid, as if they grew rabid at the sight of it.

They had been out but seventeen days, and they had thrown overboard no less than fifty-five, who had died of dysentery and other complaints, though they had left the coast in good health. Indeed, many of the survivors were seen lying about the decks in the last stage of emaciation and in a state of filth and misery not to be looked at. Even-handed justice had visited the effects of this unholy traffic on the crew. Eight or nine had died, and at that moment six were in hammocks on board, in different stages of fever. This mortality did not arise from want of medicine. There was a large stock ostentatiously displayed in the cabin, with a manuscript book containing directions as to the quantities; but the only medical man on board to prescribe it was as ignorant as his patients.

VICTORIA BECOMES QUEEN

I am very young and perhaps in many, though not in all things, inexperienced, but I am sure that very few have more real good-will and more real desire to do what is fit and right than I have

WITNESSED BY
QUEEN VICTORIA
AND CHARLES GREVILLE

When King William IV of England died of pneumonia on 20 June, 1837, he was succeeded by his niece Victoria, who was the daughter of Edward Duke of Kent (1767-1820). Princess Victoria had been the childless king's heir apparent since her birth in 1819; she knew she would be queen.

THE WITNESSES

1) Victoria lived with her mother, the widowed Duchess of Kent, at Kensington Palace in London. It was there that she was awakened by her mother to be informed of her accession to the throne, just four hours after William IV's death. The young queen lived very much under her mother's thumb, even to the extent of being made to sleep in the same bedroom. Her diary references to seeing her visitors *alone* are highly significant; she was suddenly aware that she could assert her independence. The Duchess hoped to increase her control over affairs once

her daughter was queen, even lobbying to be made regent. Victoria's determination to see officials on her own was a very pointed signal to her mother that the duchess's reign was over.

2) Charles Greville was Clerk of the Privy Council.

The Reign of Queen Victoria

The reign of Queen Victoria is generally associated with industrial expansion, grandeur and empire. Incredible developments in the spheres of science and technology revolutionized life in Britain. The railways were built, the Suez Canal constructed and opened and the telephone invented, as was the typewriter, the phonograph, incandescent lighting, the motion picture and the motor car. It was really Prince Albert, rather than Victoria herself, who encouraged and delighted in these amazing developments. It was also he who organized the Great Exhibition at

Crystal Palace, London in 1851. When Albert died of typhus fever ten years later, Victoria's life effectively came to a halt too. She went into a period of mourning that lasted for an entire decade during which she attended few public engagements and dressed all in black. She blamed her son, Edward, for her husband's death because he fell ill whilst travelling to Cambridge to confront 'Bertie' over his indiscreet behaviour. Victoria took little or no interest in technology whatsoever whilst mourning Albert's passing. She spoke into a phonograph only once, in order to bring a stop to a border dispute with the king of Ethiopia, would not even go near a type-writer and, in 1878, she dismissed Alexander Graham Bell's telephone as 'faint'.

THE WITNESS SETS THE SCENE

Queen Victoria

Tuesday, 20th June 1837. I was awoke at 6 o'clock by Mamma, who told me that the Archbishop of Canterbury and Lord Conyngham were here, and wished to see me. I got out of bed and went into my sitting-room (only in my dressing-gown) and *alone*, and saw them. Lord Conyngham (the Lord Chamberlain) then acquainted me that my poor Uncle, the King, was no more, and had expired at 12 minutes past 2 this morning, and consequently that I am *Queen*. Lord Conyngham knelt down and kissed my hand, at the same time delivering to me the official announcement of the poor King's demise. The Archbishop then told me that the Queen was desirous that he should come and tell me the details of the last moments of my poor good Uncle; he said that he had directed his mind to religion, and had died in a perfectly happy, quiet state of mind, and was quite prepared for his death. He added that the

King's sufferings at the last were not very great but that there was a good deal of uneasiness. Lord Conyngham, whom I charged to express my feelings of condolence and sorrow to the poor Queen, returned directly to Windsor. I then went to my room and dressed.

Since it has pleased Providence to place me in this station, I shall do my utmost to fulfill my duty towards my country; I am very young and perhaps in many, though not in all things, inexperienced, but I am sure that very few have more real good-will and more real desire to do what is fit and right than I have.

Character Profiles

Queen Victoria

Victoria was born on 24 May 1819 at Kensington Palace to Princess Victoria of Saxe Coburg and Edward, Duke of Kent. Her father died when Victoria was just eight months old and this perhaps explains why

Victoria and her mother, the Duchess of Kent, were so close. Her secluded childhood meant that she was given to strong prejudices and bouts of wilful stubbornness, but she was modest, straightforward and warmhearted. In 1837, when she became queen, Victoria was barely eighteen years old and determined to rule alone, without the help of her domineering mother. She continued to take her role as queen extremely seriously throughout her life.

Princess Victoria of Saxe Coburg, The Duchess of Kent

Marie Louise Victoria of Saxe Coburg Saalfeld was born in 1786. She became the Duchess of Kent in 1818 when she married Prince Edward Augustus, who would become Queen Victoria's father. When her husband died, the duchess had little reason to remain in England. She did not even speak English. But the succession was insecure at this point; her late husband had three brothers, all of whom had stronger claims to the British throne, but they were all childless. The duchess decided to stay in Britain to support the succession of her daughter, through whom she appears to have hoped to rule alongside her lover, Sir John Conroy.

....

Lord Melbourne

William Lamb, Lord Melbourne, was born in London in 1779. He was educated at Eton and Trinity College Cambridge before becoming a lawyer. As a young man he became part of the group of radical writers and thinkers that included Percy Bysshe Shelley, William Hazlitt, Henry Brougham, Lord Byron and Thomas Barnes. Brougham and Lamb went into politics, while the others became writers. He was not a particularly ambitious man, and had to be persuaded to become prime minister. Three years later, when he met the young Queen Victoria,

Lamb had just lost his wife and child, and he and the young queen developed a strong bond – rather like that of father and daughter. Lamb spent hours at a time with Victoria, and the two became such close friends that some people began to question whether the relationship was 'commonly decent' – some even referred to her as 'Mrs Melbourne'.

Baron Stockmar

Christian Freidrich Stockmar, Baron von Stockmar was a German statesman, born in Coburg in 1787. As a young man he trained as a doctor, and he became a physician to Prince Leopold in 1816. Stockmar came from a noble family of Swedish origin. It was his role as Leopold's physician that first brought Stockmar into the company of Prince Albert. Leopold also recommended the services of Stockmar to his niece, Victoria, as her personal Politics tutor, and it was Stockmar and Leopold together who eventually orchestrated the match between Albert and Victoria. Although he seemed to have stayed very much in the background, Stockmar had a great deal of influence in the upper echelons of European society at this time. He certainly had the ear of some of its most powerful leaders, and in many ways he helped to lay down the foundations of Victoria's reign.

THE WITNESSES' ACCOUNTS

1) Queen Victoria

Breakfasted, during which time good, faithful Stockmar [Baron Stockmar - a friend] came and talked to me. Wrote a letter to dear Uncle Leopold [King of the Belgians] and a few words to dear good Feodore [Victoria's step-sister]. Received a letter from Lord Melbourne [the Prime Minister] in which he said he would wait upon me at a little before 9. At 9 came Lord Melbourne, whom

I saw in my room, and of *course quite alone*, as I shall *always* do all my Ministers. He kissed my hand, and I then acquainted him that it had long been my intention to retain him and the rest of the present Ministry at the head of affairs, and that it could not be in better hands than his. He again then kissed my hand. He then read to me the Declaration which I was to read to the Council, which he wrote himself, and which is a very fine one. I then talked with him some little time longer, after which he left me. He was in full dress. I like him very much and feel confidence in him. He is a very straightforward, honest, clever and good man. I then wrote a letter to the Queen [Adelaide, William IV's widow]. At about 11 Lord Melbourne came again to me, and spoke to me upon various subjects. At about half-past 11 I went downstairs and held a Council in the red saloon.

I went in of course quite alone and remained seated the whole time. My two Uncles, the Dukes of Cumberland and Sussex, and Lord

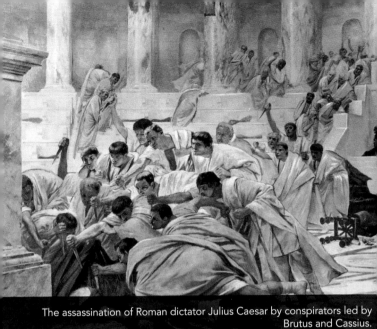

The assassination of Roman dictator Julius Caesar by conspirators led by Brutus and Cassius.

Execution of Mary Queen of Scots.

The death of Admiral Nelson.

Queen Victoria takes the sacrament at her coronation in Westminster Abbey, 28 June 1838.

The Battle of Little Bighorn.

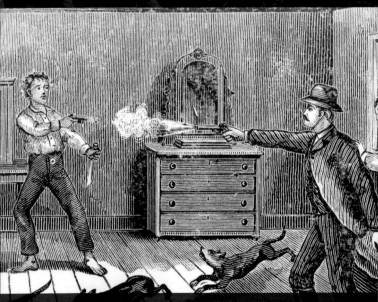

Billy the Kid meets his end at the hands of Sheriff Pat Garret, a woodcut from Beadle's half Dime Library.

A biplane designed by Wilbur and Orville Wright in flight at Sheppay, 1903.

Howard Carter emerges from the tomb of Tutankhamun, holding a box of archaeological artefacts.

Two Dornier 217 flying over the Silvertown area of London's Docklands, during the Battle of Britain.

The American destroyer USS Shaw explodes during the Japanese attack

American troops arrive on Omaha Beach, Normandy on D-Day during the invasion of Europe.

Members of the United States Marine Corps raise the American flag on Mount Suribachi on February 23, 1945 after the Battle of Iwo Jima

President and Mrs. John F. Kennedy smile at the crowds lining their motorcade route in Dallas, Texas.

The Apollo 11 Lunar Module 'Eagle' begins its ascent to rendezvous with the Command Module 'Columbia' after its successful lunar landing.

Melbourne conducted me. The Declaration, the various forms, the swearing in of the Privy Councillors of which there were a great number present, and the reception of some of the Lords of the Council, previous to the Council, in an adjacent room (likewise alone) I subjoin here. I was not at all nervous and had the satisfaction of hearing that people were satisfied with what I had done and how I had done it. Received after this, audiences of Lord Melbourne, Lord John Russell, Lord Albemarle (Master of the Horse), and the Archbishop of Canterbury, all in my room and alone. Saw Stockmar. Saw Clark, whom I named my Physician. Saw Mary. Wrote to Uncle Ernest. Saw Ernest Hohenlohe, who brought me a kind and very feeling letter from the poor Queen. I feel very much for her, and really feel that the poor good King was always so kind personally to me, that I should be ungrateful were I not to recollect it and feel grieved at his death. The poor Queen is wonderfully composed now, I hear.

Wrote my journal. Took my dinner upstairs alone.

Went downstairs. Saw Stockmar. At about twenty minutes to 9 came Lord Melbourne and remained till near 10. I had a very important and a very *comfortable* conversation with him. Each time I see him I feel more confidence in him; I find him very kind in his manner too. Saw Stockmar. Went down and said good-night to Mamma, etc. My *dear* Lehzen [Victoria's girlhood governess] will *always* remain with me as my friend, but will take no situation about me, and I think she is right.

2) Charles Greville

The actors in the ceremonial [the coronation] were very imperfect in their parts and had neglected to rehearse them. Nobody knew what was to be done except the Archbishop, Lord John Thynne, Lord Willoughby (who is experienced in these matters) and the Duke of Wellington, and consequently there was continual difficulty and embarrassment and the Queen never knew what she was to do next. When the orb was put into her hand, she said, 'What am I to do with it?'

'Your majesty is to carry it, if you please, in your hand.' 'Am I? It is very heavy.'

RACIST MURDERS BY THE KU KLUX KLAN

They told him that his time has come and if he wants to tell his wife goodbye and say his prayers – hurry up

WITNESSED BY BEN JOHNSON

When the Ku Klux Klan started in December 1865 it was a harmless social club, set up by six young men living in the village of Pulaski near Nashville, Tennessee. The men were veterans of the Confederate Army and some of them had been to college where fraternities with three-letter, Greek-based names were popular. They decided on the alliterative, non-Greek, title Ku Klux Klan. Meetings were to be held in secret and club members would disguise themselves; they would wear a sheet, a mask and a pointed hat to make them look taller. The Klan leader would be known as the Grand Cyclops.

The frightening appearance of these white-sheeted figures on horseback made the recently freed black slaves run for cover. Then deliberately terrorizing these frightened black people became a game. Then the Klan changed from being a social club to a cruel and ruthless hunting pack. After the South's defeat in the recent Civil War conditions there were chaotic. Many poor whites in the South feared that there might be an insurrection of freed slaves; their paranoia was heightened by the arrival of white 'carpet-baggers' from the North. The Klan's violent night raids were usually directed against these carpet-baggers or freed slaves, and the victims often died.

There was widespread revulsion at the atrocities committed by the Ku Klux Klan, and local authorities took action to stamp them out. Its power was already diminishing by 1868. In 1871, the US Congress passed a Ku Klux Klan Act, authorizing the use of federal troops to suppress the Klan and put its members on trial in federal court. The Klan died out, but was revived in 1915.

THE WITNESS

Ben Johnson was born a slave in the South around the year 1848. He was interviewed at the age of 85 in North Carolina by a team from the Federal Writers' Project to collect reminiscences of former slaves. He encountered the Ku Klux Klan just after the end of the Civil War.

THE WITNESS'S ACCOUNT

I was born in Orange County [North Carolina] and I belonged to Mr Gilbert Gregg near Hillsboro. I don't know nothing about my mammy and daddy, but I had a brother Jim who was sold to dress young misses for her wedding. The tree is still standing where I sat under and watch them sell Jim. I sat there and I cried and cried, especially when they put the chains on him and carried him off, and I ain't never felt so lonesome in my whole life. I ain't never hear from Jim since and I wonder now sometimes if he's still living.

I knows that the master was good to us and he fed and clothed us good. We had our own garden and we was getting along all right.

I saw a whole heap of Yankees when they came to

Hillsboro and most of them ain't got no respect for God, man, nor the devil. I can't remember so much about them though cause we lives in town - and we has a guard.

The most that I can tell you about is the Ku Klux. I never will forget when they hung Cy Guy. They hung him for a scandalous insult to a white woman and they came after him a hundred strong.

They tries him there in the woods, and they scratches Cy's arm to get some blood, and with that blood they wrote that he shall hang between the heavens and the earth till he is dead, dead, dead, and that any nigger what takes down the body shall be hanged too.

Well sir, the next morning there he hung, right over the road and the sentence hanging over his head. Nobody would bother with that body for four days and there it hung, swinging in the wind, but the fourth day the sheriff comes and takes it down.

There was Ed and Cindy, who before the war belonged to Mr Lynch and after the war he told them to move. He gave them a month and they ain't gone, so the Ku Kluxes got them.

It was on a cold night when they came and dragged the niggers out of bed. They carried them down in the woods and whipped them, then they threw them in the pond, their bodies breaking the ice. Ed came out and came to our house, but Cindy ain't been seen since.

Sam Allen in Caswell County was told to move and after a month the hundred Ku Klux came a-toting his casket and they told him that his time has come and if he wants to tell his wife goodbye and say his prayers - hurry up.

They set the coffin on two chairs and Sam kissed his old woman who was crying, then he knelt down beside his bed with his head on the pillow and his arms thrown out in front of him.

He sat there for a minute and when he rose he

had a long knife in his hand. Before he could be grabbed, he killed two of the Ku Kluxes with the knife, and he went out of the door. They didn't catch him either, and the next night when they came back, determined to get him, they shot another nigger by accident.

Bob Boylan falls in love with another woman, so he burned his wife and four youngsters up in their house. The Ku Kluxes got him, of course, and they hanged him high on the old red oak on the Hillsboro Road. After they hanged him, his lawyer said to us boys: 'Bury him good, boys, just as good as you'd bury me if I was dead'. I shook hands with Bob before they hanged him and I helped bury him too and we buried him nice and we all hoped that he done gone to glory.

THE BATTLE OF THE LITTLE BIGHORN

At the peep of day the Indians opened a heavy fire and a desperate fight ensued

WITNESSED BY
GEORGE HERENDON

The US Army was determined to force a large Indian army back to the reservations. There were three columns, one of which contained Lieut-Colonel George Custer and the Seventh Cavalry. On June 25, 1876, Custer sighted a Sioux encampment and a nearby group of 40 warriors. He decided to attack before realizing he was outnumbered three-to-one. Custer divided his forces, sending some men under Captain Benteen to prevent the Indians escaping through the upper valley. Major Reno was to cross the Little Bighorn River and charge the Indian village with the remaining troops under his command. Custer's plan was to strike the Indian camp from both sides at once, but had no idea what kind of terrain he would have to cross. He discovered, too late, that it was a maze of bluffs and ravines.

Reno's squadron attacked the southern end, then retreated uphill, hotly pursued by Cheyenne and Sioux. Then the Indians found Custer's men coming towards the other end of the village. Cheyenne and Sioux together crossed the river and forced Custer back up a ridge to the north. Meanwhile, another force under Crazy Horse doubled back to surround and trap Custer.

In less than an hour, Custer and his men were massacred in one of the worst American military disasters.

THE WITNESS

George Herendon served as a civilian scout for the Seventh Cavalry and was attached to Major Reno's command. Herendon told his story to the *New York Herald*.

THE WITNESS'S ACCOUNT

Reno took a steady gallop and found a natural ford across the Little Bighorn River. He started to cross, when the scouts came back and called out to him to hold on, that the Sioux were coming in large numbers to meet him. He crossed over, however, formed his companies on the prairie in line of battle, and moved forward at a trot but soon took a gallop.

He advanced about a mile from the ford to a line of timber on the right and dismounted his men to fight on foot. The horses were sent into the timber, and the men forward on the prairie and advanced toward the Indians. The Indians, mounted on ponies, came across the prairie and opened fire on the soldiers. After skirmishing for a few minutes Reno fell back to his horses in the timber. The Indians moved to his left and rear, evidently with the intention of cutting him off from the ford.

Reno ordered his men to mount and move through the timber, but as his men got into the saddle the Sioux, who had advanced in the timber, fired at close range and killed one soldier. Colonel Reno then commanded the men to dismount, and they did so, but he soon ordered them to mount again, and moved out on to the open prairie.

The command headed for the ford. The Sioux,

mounted on their swift ponies, dashed up by the side of the soldiers and fired at them, killing both men and horses. Little resistance was offered, and it was complete rout to the ford. I did not see the men at the ford, and do not know what took place further than a good many were killed when the command left the timber.

Just as I got out, my horse stumbled and fell and I was dismounted, the horse running away after Reno's command. I saw several soldiers who were dismounted, their horses having been killed or run away. There were also some soldiers mounted who had remained behind, I should think in all thirteen soldiers, and seeing no chance of getting away I called on them to come into the timber and we would stand off the Indians.

Three of the soldiers were wounded, and two of them so badly they could not use their arms. The soldiers wanted to go out, but I said no, we can't get to the ford, and besides, we have wounded men and must stand by them. The soldiers still wanted to go, but I told them I was an old frontiers-man, understood the Indians, and if they would do as I said I would get them out of the scrape. About half of the men were mounted, and they wanted to keep their horses with them, but I told them to let the horses go and fight on foot.

....

"Three of the soldiers were wounded, and two of them so badly they could not use their arms"

....

We stayed in the bush about three hours, and I could hear heavy firing apparently about two miles distant. I did not know who it was, but knew the Indians were fighting some of our men, and learned afterward it was Custer's command. Nearly all the Indians in the upper part of the valley drew off down the river, and the fight with Custer lasted about one hour, when the heavy firing ceased. When the shooting below began to die away I said to the boys, 'Come, now is the time to get out.' Most of them did not go, but waited for night. I told them the Indians would come back and we had better be off at once. Eleven of the thirteen said they would go, but two stayed behind.

I deployed the men as skirmishers and we moved forward on foot toward the river. When we had got nearly to the river we met five Indians on ponies, and they fired on us. I returned the fire and the Indians broke and we then forded the river, the water being heart deep. We finally got over, wounded men and all, and headed for Reno's command which I could see drawn up on the bluffs along the river about a mile off. We reached Reno in safety.

We had not been with Reno more than fifteen minutes when I saw the Indians coming up the valley from Custer's fight.[1] Reno moved his command down the ridge toward Custer. The

1 – Custer's fight became legendary as 'Custer's Last Stand'.

Indians crossed the river below Reno and swarmed up the bluff on all sides. After skirmishing with them Reno went back to his old position which was on one of the highest fronts along the bluffs. It was now about five o'clock, and the fight lasted until it was too dark to see to shoot.

As soon as it was dark Reno took the packs and saddles off the mules and horses and made breast works of them. He also dragged the dead horses and mules on the line and sheltered the men behind them.

At the peep of day the Indians opened a heavy fire and a desperate fight ensued, lasting until 10 o'clock. The Indians charged our position three or four times, coming up close enough to hit our men with stones. Captain Benteen saw a large mass of Indians gathered on his front to charge, and ordered his men to charge on foot and scatter them.

Benteen led the charge and was upon the Indians before they knew what they were about and killed a great many. They were evidently much surprised at this offensive movement, and I think in desperate fighting Benteen is one of the bravest men I ever saw. He never sheltered his own person once during the battle, and I do not see how he escaped being killed. The desperate charging and fighting was over at about one o'clock.

THE DEATH OF BILLY THE KID

He wore a broad-brimmed hat, a dark vest and pants, and was in his shirtsleeves...little as we then suspected it, this man was the Kid.

WITNESSED BY
PAT GARRETT

Billy The Kid was born in the New York slums in 1859. After his father died, he travelled west with his mother, ending up in New Mexico in 1873. He turned up in Lincoln County, New Mexico, in 1877 – under the name of William Bonney. Lincoln County was in a lawless state in 1877. The native Apache had recently been subdued and the local cattlemen divided themselves into two camps in a fight for local power. Billy the Kid allied himself with the losing side in the Lincoln County War, working as a ranch hand for John Tunstall, a leader of one of the factions. Tunstall befriended the Kid, who regarded him as a surrogate father. Tunstall's ambush and murder in 1878 by a sheriff's posse gave the Kid a thirst for revenge.

His first victims were the sheriff and his deputy, killed in an ambush on the streets of Lincoln. The Kid was on the run for two years before being captured (by Garrett), tried, convicted and returned to Lincoln for execution. But Lincoln's jail was no match for Billy the Kid.

On the evening of 28 April, 1881 as he was being returned to his cell, the Kid grabbed a gun and shot his guard. A second guard ran from across the street when he heard the shots, only to be shot down by the Kid from the balcony above. In true Western style, Billy the Kid mounted a horse and galloped out of town.

THE WITNESS

Pat Garrett was elected Sheriff of Lincoln County in 1880; he was expected to reinstate justice in the area. One of his first acts was to capture Billy the Kid, in order that he should stand trial for the murder of the Lincoln sheriff and his deputy. While Garrett was away on business, Billy the Kid made his escape. Instead of pursuing the fugitive, Garrett stayed on his ranch mending fences and tending his livestock. In July 1880, Garrett heard that the Kid was hiding out at the abandoned Fort Sumner about 140 miles away. Garrett set off in pursuit with two deputies, John Poe and Thomas McKinney.

On the night of July 14, the Sheriff and his two deputies approached the abandoned fort, now converted to living quarters. The residents were sympathetic to the Kid and the lawmen could extract little information. Garrett decided to seek out an old friend, Peter Maxwell, who might tell him the Kid's whereabouts. By chance, the Kid stumbled right into the Sheriff's hands. Garrett published his account of the incident a year after it happened.

THE WITNESS SETS THE SCENE

I then concluded to go and have a talk with Peter Maxwell, Esq, in whom I felt sure I could rely. We had ridden to within a short distance of Maxwell's grounds when we found a man in camp and stopped. To Poe's great surprise, he recognized in the camper an old friend and former partner, in Texas, named Jacobs. We unsaddled here, got some coffee, and, on foot, entered an orchard which runs from this point down to a row of old buildings, some of them occupied by Mexicans, not more than sixty yards from Maxwell's house.

Character Profiles

Billy the Kid

Billy the Kid was born Henry McCarty on 17 September 1859, in New York City. His father, Patrick McCarty, died in 1863, and the family moved to Wichita in order to find a warm dry climate for his mother, who was suffering from tuberculosis. His mother remarried a man named William Antrim, but she died in 1874. It was about this time that the now orphaned Henry McCarty became Billy the Kid. The Kid's reputation rests largely on the fact that he was a master escape artist, and escaping is something he had plenty of practice at. His first arrest came in 1875, when he was captured for taking part in the robbery of a Chinese laundry. He managed to escape through a fireplace chimney and fled to Arizona, where his crime spree continued unabated. In August 1877 he murdered Frank Cahil, a bullying blacksmith at Fort Grant. He was arrested for the killing but escaped from jail once again.

The event that eventually led to his downfall was the murder of Billy's friend, John Tunstall, who he regarded as a father figure. At John's funeral, Billy vowed to kill every man who had a hand in the murder, and this is exactly what he set out to do. It was later claimed that Billy the Kid killed a man for every 21 years of his life, but historians now think that he was actually responsible for the deaths of somewhere between four and nine people.

Pat Garrett

Pat Garrett was born in Chambers County, Alabama on 5 June, 1850. One of seven children belonging to farmers John Lumpkin Garrett and his wife Elizabeth Ann Jarvis Garrett. The family moved to a plantation in Louisiana and, following a brief spell of schooling, he left Louisiana to become a trail driver and buffalo hunter in Texas. When the slaughter of buffalos became unprofitable, Garrett moved to New Mexico and married Apolinaria Gutierrez. On 2 November 1880, Garrett, a democrat, was elected sheriff of Lincoln County. During his campaign he had vowed to put a stop to the current reign of lawlessness in the region, now he was charged with tracking down and bringing to justice the area's most notorious outlaw – Billy the Kid.

THE WITNESS'S ACCOUNT

We approached these houses cautiously, and when within earshot, heard the sound of voices conversing in Spanish. We concealed ourselves quickly and listened; but the distance was too great to hear words, or even distinguish voices. Soon a man arose from the ground, in full view, but too far away to recognize. He wore a broad-brimmed hat, a dark vest and pants, and was in his shirtsleeves. With a few words, which fell like a murmur on our ears, he went to the fence, jumped it, and walked down towards Maxwell's house.

Little as we then suspected it, this man was the Kid. We learned, subsequently, that, when he left his companions that night, he went to the house of a Mexican friend, pulled off his hat and boots, threw himself on a bed, and commenced reading a newspaper. He soon, however, hailed his friend, who was sleeping in the room, told him to get up and make some coffee, adding: 'Give me a butcher knife and I will go over to Pete's and get some beef; I'm hungry.' The Mexican arose, handed him the knife, and the Kid, hatless and in his stocking-feet, started to Maxwell's, which was but a few steps distant.

When the Kid, by me unrecognized, left the orchard, I motioned to my companions, and we cautiously retreated a short distance, and, to avoid the persons whom we had heard at the houses, took another route, approaching Maxwell's house from the opposite direction. When we reached the porch in front of the building, I left Poe and McKinney at the end of the porch, about twenty feet from the door of Pete's room, and went in. It was near midnight and Pete was in bed. I walked to the head of the bed and sat down on it, beside him, near the pillow. I asked him as to the whereabouts of the Kid. He said that the Kid had certainly been about, but he did not know whether he had left or not. At that moment a man sprang quickly into the door, looking back, and called twice in Spanish, 'Who comes there?'

No one replied and he came on in. He was bareheaded. From his step I could perceive he was either barefooted or in his stocking-feet, and held a revolver in his right hand and a butcher knife in his left.

....

"I could perceive he was either barefooted or in his stocking-feet, and held a revolver in his right hand and a butcher knife in his left"

....

He came directly towards me. Before he reached the bed, I whispered: 'Who is it, Pete?' but received no reply for a moment. It struck me that it might be Pete's brother-in-law, Manuel Abreu, who had seen Poe and McKinney, and wanted to know their business. The intruder came close to me, leaned both hands on the bed, his right hand almost touching my knee, and asked, in a low tone, 'Who are they, Pete?' At the same instant Maxwell whispered to me, 'That's him!'

Simultaneously the Kid must have seen, or felt, the presence of a third person at the head of the bed. He raised quickly his pistol, a self-cocker, within a foot of my breast. Retreating rapidly across the room he cried: 'Quien es? Quien es?' (Who's that? Who's that?) All this occurred in a moment. Quickly as possible I drew my revolver and fired, threw my body aside, and fired again. The second shot was useless; the Kid fell dead. He never spoke. A struggle or two, a little strangling sound as he gasped for breath, and the Kid was with his many victims.

Law and Order in the Wild West

The strangest thing about law and order in the Wild West was that outlaws and lawmen were often interchangeable. A lawman in one state might well have been a bandit in another. Indeed, Pat Garrett himself had a murky past, which involved killing a man during a hunting dispute. Even one of the most famous lawmen of the Wild West, Bill Tilgham, did not start out as a good guy. He was arrested for theft as a young man, before being appointed city marshal of Dodge

THE DEATH OF BILLY THE KID

in 1884. This exchange could also happen the other way around. Burton Alvord was the son of a justice of the peace, and at the age of 20 he became a deputy sheriff of Cochise county, where he gained a reputation as an excellent tracker. This reputation as an efficient lawman started to slip when Burton began to drink heavily and socialise with known outlaws. This bad crowd eventually persuaded him to turn to the dark side, and Burton became a cattle rustler just like many of his ne'er-do-well friends. With the gap between good and evil considerably narrowed, which side you were fighting on often came down to who offered the biggest reward. Billy the Kid sold many of his closest friends down the river when he thought it might save him from the gallows, and the chances are that Pat Garrett was motivated as much by the $500 reward that was offered in exchange for the life of Billy the Kid as he was by his duty as sheriff.

THE FIRST POWERED FLIGHT

At just 12 o'clock Will started on the fourth and last trip. The machine started off with its ups and downs as it had before, but by the time he had gone over three or four hundred feet he had it under much better control

WITNESSED BY
ORVILLE WRIGHT

On 17 December, 1903, Orville Wright piloted the first powered plane at an altitude of just 20 feet over a wind-swept beach in North Carolina. The flight lasted just 12 seconds and covered 120 feet. Three more flights were made that day, Orville's brother Wilbur piloting the record flight, which lasted 59 seconds over a distance of 852 feet.

The brothers notified the press before their historic flight. No major newspaper reported the event.

THE WITNESS

Orville Wright (1871-1948) was the younger of the two Wright brothers. He was 32 years old at the time of the first flight, while his brother Wilbur was 36. They were both self-taught aviation pioneers.

On the morning of 17 December, the day of the first flight, the conditions were perfect for flight at Kitty Hawk in North Carolina; the wind was strong, consistent and northerly. At about 10.30 am, Orville Wright lay down on the plane's wing surface and brought its engine to life in preparation to launch it and himself into history. His diary tells the story.

After this historic first flight, Orville and Wilbur gave up their cycle business, patented the flying machine and set up an aircraft production company.

The Pioneers of Aviation

Orville and Wilbur Wright were not the only individuals dabbling in aviation at the time of their maiden flight. For decades there had been engineers all over the developed world who were inventing flying machines and conducting experiments with varying degrees of success. Clement Ader was one such inventor. In 1890, he designed and built a steam powered, bat-winged monoplane, which he called 'Eole'. On October 9, he flew a distance of 50m (160ft) on a friend's estate, but he found that steam was not a suitable source of energy for sustained and controlled flight. He was, however, the first man to take off in a manned heavier-than-air craft using only its own power. An English baronet, Sir George Cayley, is sometimes referred to as the 'Father of Aviation'. A true pioneer, he was responsible for identifying the four major aeronautical forces for flight: weight, lift, drag and thrust. His second major aviation break-through involved designing the first successful human-carrying glider. Two British industrialists, Henson and Stringfellow, were inspired by the writings of Cayley to design and build the 'Ariel', a design which was patented in 1842. The Ariel design also proved to be prophetic of later, more successful, aircraft design, but it was also powered by steam engine – albeit a very light one. Henson and Stringfellow dreamt of founding a commercial international airline, called Aerial Transit Company. They began raising investment capital and even embarked on a publicity campaign. Unfortunately the Ariel, and many different incarnations of Ariel, simply failed to fly.

THE WITNESS SETS THE SCENE

When we got up, a wind of between 20 and 25 miles [per hour] was blowing from the north. We got the machine out early and put out the signal for the men at the station. Before we were quite ready, John T. Daniels, W. S. Dough, A. D. Etheridge, W. C. Brinkley of Manteo, and Johnny Moore of Nags Head arrived.

After running the engine and propellers a few minutes to get them in working order, I got on the machine at 10.35 for the first trial. The wind, according to our anemometers at this time, was blowing a little over 20 miles (corrected) 27 miles according to the Government anemometer at

Kitty Hawk. On slipping the rope the machine started off increasing in speed to probably 7 or 8 miles [per hour]. The machine lifted from the truck just as it was entering on the fourth rail. Mr Daniels took a picture just as it left the tracks.

Character Profiles

Orville Wright

Orville Wright was born on 19 August 1871 in Dayton, Ohio. Orville said he and his siblings were lucky enough to be encouraged to express themselves freely and investigate whatever subject aroused their curiosity. The two libraries in the Wright household also helped facilitate academic learning, but Orville was the more boisterous of the two Wright brothers. He preferred typically adventurous boys' pursuits, such as cycling, to excessive studying. It was a result of Orville's passion for cycling that he and Wilbur entered the bicycle business together, a step which led directly to the beginning of aviation.

....

Wilbur Wright

Wilbur Wright, in contrast with his brother, Orville, was more intellectually motivated. He excelled in school, had an excellent memory and was a good athlete too. He was a calm and collected person with a steady demeanour. His father, Milton, once said that he was 'never rattled in thought or temper'. This was probably of major advantage to the Wright brothers in their experiments with air travel. Wilbur had the patience and determination and Orville had the vitality and passion to see a plan to its ultimate conclusion. Wilbur was left with health complications following a childhood ice hockey accident, and this had the effect of making him withdraw from the outside world for a time. During this difficult period, Wilbur gave up his plan to attend Yale University and become a teacher, and focused instead on finding a career closer to home. If Wilbur had gone to Yale as originally intended, the chances are that he would not have been in a position to go into business with his brother Orville, and the story of the birth of aviation would have developed differently.

THE WITNESS'S ACCOUNT

I found the control of the front rudder quite difficult on account of its being balanced too near the centre and thus had a tendency to turn itself when started so that the rudder was turned too far on one side and then too far on the other. As a result the machine would rise suddenly to about 10 feet and then as suddenly, on turning the rudder, dart for the ground. A sudden dart when out about 100 feet from the end of the tracks ended the flight. Time about 12 seconds (not known exactly as watch was not promptly stopped). The lever for throwing off the engine was broken, and the skid under the rudder cracked. After repairs, at 20 min. after 11 o'clock Will [Wilbur Wright] made the second trial.

The course was about like mine, up and down but a little longer over the ground though about the same in time. Dist. not measured but about 175 ft. Wind speed not quite so strong. With the aid of the station men present, we picked the machine up and carried it back to the starting ways. At about 20 minutes till 12 o'clock I made the third trial. When out about the same distance as Will's, I met with a strong gust from the left which raised the left wing and sidled the machine off to the right in a lively manner. I immediately turned the rudder to bring the machine down and then worked the end control. Much to our surprise, on reaching the ground the left wing struck first, showing the lateral control of this machine much more effective than on any of our former ones. At the time of its sidling it had raised to a height of probably 12 to 14 feet.

....

"it began its pitching again and suddenly darted into the ground"

....

At just 12 o'clock Will started on the fourth and last trip. The machine started off with its ups and downs as it had before, but by the time he had gone over three or four hundred feet he had it under much better control, and was travelling on a fairly even course. It proceeded in this manner till it reached a small hummock out about 800 feet from the starting ways, when it began its pitching again and suddenly darted into the ground.

The front rudder frame was badly broken up, but the main frame suffered none at all. The distance over the ground was 852 feet in 59 seconds. The engine turns was 1071, but this included several seconds while on the starting ways and probably about a half second after landing. The jar of landing had set the watch on machine back so that we have no exact record for the 1071 turns. Will took a picture of my third flight just before the gust struck the machine.

The machine left the ways successfully at every trial, and the tail was never caught by the truck as we had feared.

After removing the front rudder, we carried the machine back to camp. We set the machine down a few feet west of the building, and while standing about discussing the last flight, a sudden gust of wind struck the machine and started to turn it over. All rushed to stop it. Will who was near one end ran to the front, but too late to do any good. Mr Daniels and myself seized spars at the rear, but to no purpose. The machine gradually turned over on us. Mr. Daniels, having had no experience in handling a machine of this kind, hung on to it from the inside, and as a result was knocked down and turned over and over with it as it went. His escape was miraculous, as he was in with the engine and chains. The engine legs were all broken off, the chain guides badly bent, a number of uprights, and nearly all the rear ends of the ribs were broken. One spar only was broken.

REACHING THE SOUTH POLE

I am just going outside and may be some time

WITNESSED BY
CAPTAIN ROBERT FALCON SCOTT

A British team led by Captain Scott set out in January 1911 to reach the South Pole. They discovered they were in a race with a Norwegian expedition led by Roald Amundsen. As Scott approached the South Pole on 16 January 1912, he and his men were deeply disappointed to find evidence that Amundsen had beaten them – the Norwegians' sledge tracks. In fact Amundsen reached the South Pole on 14 December 1911, a whole month before Scott reached it on 17 January 1912.

THE WITNESS

Captain Robert Falcon Scott, the expedition leader, kept a diary. It was found by a search party on 12 November 1912, along with the bodies of Scott, Henry Bowers and Edward Wilson, in the tent where they had died of starvation, exhaustion and hypothermia eight months earlier, on 30 March 1912. They had been on their way back to their home base from the pole, numb with a sense of failure.

THE WITNESS'S ACCOUNT

Wednesday, January 17 - Camp 69. T. -22 degrees [Fahrenheit] at start. Night -21 degrees. The Pole. Yes, but under very different circumstances from those expected. We have had a horrible day - add to our disappointment a head wind 4 to 5 [miles per hour], with a temperature -22 degrees, and companions labouring on with cold feet and hands. We started at 7.30, none of us having slept much after the shock of our discovery. We followed the Norwegian sledge tracks for some way; as far as we make out there are only two men. In about three miles we passed two small cairns. Then the weather overcast, and the tracks being increasingly drifted up and obviously going too far to the West, we decided to make straight for the Pole according to our calculations. We have been descending again, I think, but there looks to be a rise ahead; otherwise there is very little that is different from the awful monotony of past days. Great God! this is an awful place and terrible enough for us to have laboured to it without the reward of priority. Well, it is something to have got here, and the wind may be our friend to-morrow. Now for the run home and a desperate struggle. I wonder if we can do it.

Thursday morning, January 18 - Well, we have turned our back now on the goal of our ambition and must face our 800 miles of solid dragging - and good-bye to most of the day-dreams!

Saturday, February 17 - A very terrible day. Evans looked a little better after a good sleep, and declared, as he always did, that he was quite well. He started in his place on the traces, but half an hour later worked his ski shoes adrift, and had to leave the sledge. We stopped after about one hour, and Evans came up again, but very slowly. Half an hour later he dropped out again on the same plea. I cautioned him to come on as quickly as he could, and he answered cheerfully as I thought. We had to push on, and the remainder of us were forced to pull very hard, sweating heavily. Abreast the Monument Rock we stopped, and seeing Evans a long way astern, I camped for lunch. There was no alarm at first, and we prepared tea and our own meal, consuming the latter.

After lunch, and Evans still not appearing, we looked out, to see him still afar off. By this time we were alarmed, and all four started back on ski. I was first to reach the poor man and shocked at his appearance; he was on his knees with clothing disarranged, hands uncovered and frostbitten, and a wild look in his eyes. Asked what was the matter, he replied with a slow speech that he didn't know, but thought he must have fainted. We got him on his feet, but after two or three steps he sank down again. He showed every sign of complete collapse. Wilson, Bowers, and I went back for the sledge, whilst Oates remained with him. When we returned he was practically unconscious, and when we got him into the tent quite comatose. He died quietly at 12.30 a.m. On discussing the symptoms we think he began to get weaker just before we reached the Pole, and that his downward path was accelerated first by the shock of his frostbitten fingers, and later by falls during rough travelling on the glacier, further by his loss of all confidence in himself. Wilson thinks it certain he must have injured his brain by a fall...

Friday, March 16 or Saturday 17 - Lost track of dates, but think the last correct. Tragedy all along the line. At lunch, the day before yesterday, poor Titus Oates said he couldn't go on; he proposed we should leave him in his sleeping-bag. That we could not do, and we induced him to come on, on the afternoon march. In spite of its awful nature for him he struggled on and we made a few miles. At night he was worse and we knew the end had come.

Should this be found I want these facts recorded. Oates' last thoughts were of his Mother, but immediately before he took pride in thinking that his regiment would be pleased with the bold way in which he met his death. We can testify to his bravery. He did not - would not - give up hope till the very end. He was a brave soul. This was the end. He slept through the night before last, hoping not to wake; but he woke in the morning - yesterday. It was blowing a blizzard. He said, 'I am just going outside and may be some time.' He went out into the blizzard and we have not seen him since.

Wednesday, March 21 - Got within 11 miles of depot Monday night; had to lay up all yesterday in severe blizzard. Today forlorn hope, Wilson and Bowers going to depot for fuel.

Thursday, March 22 and 23 - Blizzard bad as ever - Wilson and Bowers unable to start - tomorrow last chance - no fuel and only one or two of food left - must be near the end. Have decided it shall be natural - we shall march for the depot with or without our effects and die in our tracks.

Thursday, March 29 - Since the 21st we have had a continuous gale from WSW and SW. We had fuel to make two cups of tea apiece and bare food for two days on the 20th. Every day we have been ready to start for our depot 11 miles away, but outside the door of the tent it remains a scene of whirling drift. I do not think we can hope for any better things now. We shall stick it out to the end, but we are getting weaker, of course, and the end cannot be far. It seems a pity, but I do not think I can write more.

R. Scott

For God's sake look after our people.

CHRISTMAS IN THE TRENCHES

One of their men, speaking in English, mentioned that he had worked in Brighton for some years and that he was fed up to the neck with this damned war

WITNESSED BY
FRANK RICHARDS

In November 1914 the German advance across Belgium was checked by the Allies before it could reach Paris. The enemies stared at each other across a barbed-wire no man's land that in places was only 30 metres (100 feet) wide. The misery of trench warfare was intensified by the winter weather. To make matters worse, many of the trenches, especially the low-lying British trenches, were flooded most of the time.

The misery was briefly interrupted by a spontaneous Christmas Truce that started on Christmas Eve. It was the German soldiers who made the first move. They delivered a chocolate cake to the British line with a note proposing a cease-fire to allow the Germans to have a concert. The British agreed, offering a present of tobacco to the Germans. The seasonal goodwill spread along the entire 48 km (30 miles) of the British line. The men shouted to each other from the trenches, sang songs and even met in the middle of no man's land to talk and play football.

Senior officers on both sides frowned on this fraternization, and stopped it, though in some places it went on into January.

In the four years of the First World War it only happened once.

THE WITNESS

Frank Richards was one of the British soldiers who joined in the Christmas Truce.

THE WITNESS'S ACCOUNT

On Christmas morning we stuck up a board with 'A Merry Christmas' on it. The enemy had stuck up a similar one. Platoons would sometimes go out for twenty-four hours' rest - it was a day at least out of the trench and relieved the monotony a bit - and my platoon had gone out in this way the night before, but a few of us stayed behind to see what would happen. Two of our men then threw their equipment off and jumped on the parapet with their hands above their heads. Two of the Germans done the same and commenced to walk up the river bank, our two men going to meet them. They met and shook hands and then we all got out of the trench.

Buffalo Bill [the Company Commander] rushed into the trench and endeavoured to prevent it, but he was too late: the whole of the Company were now out, and so were the Germans. He had to accept the situation, so soon he and the other company officers climbed out too. We and the Germans met in the middle of no-man's-land. Their officers was also now out. Our officers exchanged greetings with them. One of the German officers said that he wished he had a camera to take a snapshot, but they were not allowed to carry cameras. Neither were our officers.

We mucked in all day with one another. They were Saxons and some of them could speak English. By the look of them their trenches were in as bad a state as our own. One of their men, speaking in English, mentioned that he had worked in Brighton for some years and that he was fed up to the neck with this damned war and would be glad when it was all over. We told him that he wasn't the only one that was fed up with it. We did not allow them in our trench and they did not allow us in theirs.

The German Company-Commander asked Buffalo Bill if he would accept a couple of barrels of beer and assured him that they would not make his men drunk. They had plenty of it in the brewery. He accepted the offer with thanks and a couple of their men rolled the barrels over and we took them into our trench. The German officer sent one of his men back to the trench, who appeared shortly after carrying a tray with bottles and glasses on it. Officers of both sides clinked glasses and drunk one another's health. Buffalo Bill had presented them with a plum pudding just before. The officers came to an understanding that the unofficial truce would end at midnight. At dusk we went back to our respective trenches. The two barrels of beer were drunk, and the German officer was right: if it was possible for a man to have drunk the two barrels himself he would have burst before he had got drunk. French beer was rotten stuff.

Just before midnight we all made it up[1] not to commence firing before they did. At night there was always plenty of firing by both sides if there were no working parties or patrols out. Mr Richardson, a young officer who had just joined the Battalion and was now a platoon officer in my company, wrote a poem during the night about the Briton and the Bosche[2] meeting in no-man's-land on Christmas Day, which he read out to us. A few days later it was published in *The Times* or *Morning Post*, I believe.

During the whole of Boxing Day we never fired a shot, and they the same, each side seemed to be waiting for the other to set the ball a-rolling. One of their men shouted across in English and

1 – Agreed.
2 – British soldiers often referred to the Germans as 'the Bosche'.

inquired how we had enjoyed the beer. We shouted back and told him it was very weak but that we were very grateful for it. We were conversing off and on during the whole of the day.

We were relieved that evening at dusk by a battalion of another brigade. We were mighty surprised as we had heard no whisper of any relief during the day. We told the men who relieved us how we had spent the last couple of days with the enemy, and by what they had been told the whole of the British troops in the line, with one or two exceptions, had mucked in with the enemy. They had only been out of action themselves forty-eight hours after being twenty-eight days in the front-line trenches. They also told us that the French people had heard how we had spent Christmas Day and were saying all manner of nasty things about the British Army.

THE MURDER OF THE TSAR

We must shoot them all tonight

WITNESSED BY
PAVEL MEDVEDEV

After Tsar Nicholas II was forced to abdicate, he was replaced by a short-lived Provisional Government. Then the Bolsheviks led by Lenin seized power in St Petersburg. A civil war between Bolsheviks (Reds) and anti-Bolsheviks (Whites) developed. From the spring of 1918 the Bolsheviks held the Tsar and his family prisoner in the Ipatiev House in the town of Ekaterinburg, beyond the Urals.

In mid-July a Czech contingent of the White Army approached Ekaterinburg and the Bolsheviks feared that the Tsar might be rescued. The sound of gunfire in the distance sealed the Tsar's fate. In the early hours of 17 July 1918, the Tsar, his wife, their children and their servants were roused from sleep, told they were to assemble downstairs. There, a few minutes later, in a ground floor room, they were all murdered.

When the remains of the Tsar and his family were discovered in the 1990s, some were missing and it looked as if Alexei, the Tsar's son, and one of the daughters might have escaped. But two bodies were buried slightly apart. In 2007 they were found – Alexei and his sister Maria.

The Tsar's valet Chemadura had a lucky escape; he fell ill and was moved to the hospital, where he was apparently overlooked by the execution squad.

THE WITNESS

Pavel Medvedev was a member of the squad of soldiers responsible for guarding the Russian royal family.

THE WITNESS SETS THE SCENE

In the evening of 16 July, between seven and eight pm, when the time of my duty had just begun, Commandant Yurovsky[1], ordered me to take all the Nagan revolvers from the guards and to bring them to him. I took twelve revolvers from the sentries as well as from some other of the guards and brought them to the commandant's office.

1 – Yurovsky was a powerful figure in the Ekaterinburg Extraordinary Commission for Combating Counter-Revolution; he also headed the execution squad.

Yurovsky said to me, 'We must shoot them all tonight; so notify the guards not to be alarmed if they hear shots.' I understood, therefore, that Yurovsky had it in his mind to shoot the whole of the Tsar's family, as well as the doctor and the servants who lived with them, but I did not ask him where or by whom the decision had been made. . . At about ten o'clock in the evening in accordance with Yurovsky's order I informed the guards not to be alarmed if they should hear firing.

The Russian Revolution

The Russian Revolution of 1917 is often referred to as the Bolshevik revolution or the October revolution, but, in fact, there were two distinctly separate phases. The first happened in February 1917, when the Tsar, Nicholas II, abdicated and a provisional government took control over Russia. The second happened later that year, in October, when the Bolsheviks seized power and overthrew the provisional government. Both phases were part of a revolution to replace a regime that had exploited and oppressed the working classes for centuries. In the early twentieth century, Russian society began to change dramatically. There was increased rural-to-urban migration among workers, and the traditional class boundaries were beginning to blur. At the same time western, capitalist ideas were seeding themselves in peoples' minds, and the people began to be more politicized. They felt the Tsar was, at best, utterly out of touch with the aspirations of his subjects, and at worst, an exploitative tyrant. In January 1917, the British Ambassador to Russia, Sir George Buchanan, advised Nicholas to 'break down the barrier that separates you from your people to regain their confidence'. But the Tsar and Tsarina were staunch opponents of political reform, and they refused to entertain the idea. It was this inaction that lead to their downfall.

Character Profiles

....

Commandant Yurovsky

Yakov Mikhailovich Yurovsky was born in 1878 in Tomsk. His father, Michael, worked as a glazier, and his mother was a seamstress. Yurovsky later wrote that the two of them worked to exhaustion. With ten children to feed and clothe, they had little choice. Young Yakov began to question why some people were born into a life of hardship, whereas others had everything they wanted. Unlike the rest of his family, he did not believe that these hardships were sent from heaven to test, or to punish, people. It was these feelings of injustice that drove Yakov Yurovsky to join the Bolsheviks, he came to see the Emperer and his family as blood-sucking parasites, feeding on the lives of the poor. He was of the view that it was not in fact the worker who depended upon the royal family, but the workers who determined the fate of their rulers. In 1918, as the commandant with control over the Tsar and Tsarina's lives, as well as that of their offspring, this prophesy aquired a literal truth.

....

Tsar Nicholas II

Nikolai Aleksandrovich Romanov was born in 1868 the eldest son of Tsar Alexander III. When his father died in 1894, Nicholas succeeded as Tsar and quickly married Princess Alexandra of Hesse-Darmstadt, a German duchy. Together Nicholas and Alexandra had four daughters and one son, Alexis, who suffered from haemophilia, something he shared with his mother's relatives in England – the Saxe Coburgs. During his reign, Tsar Nicholas II faced a great many problems both from abroad and at home. On an international level, he favoured an expanded Russia and made plans to seize Constantinople. He also expanded into Manchuria and Korea. This angered the Japanese, who retaliated with surprise attacks. Nicholas II was extremely rich, yet Russian industrial workers worked 11 hours a day and 10 hours on Saturday. Conditions in the factories were harsh and little concern was given to health and safety. The trade unions were angry with the Russian authorities and the monarchy. Given the turbulent domestic situation, and Nicholas's belligerent refusal to entertain the idea of political reform, it is not difficult to see why the Bolsheviks were moved to action against the monarchy.

The Empress

Princess Alexandra was born in 1872 in Darmstadt, the sixth child of Grand Duke Louis of Hesse and the English Princess Alice of the United Kingdom. The Tsarina was often described as the dominant partner in her marriage to Tsar Nicholas II. She was a strong believer in the autocratic power of the Tsar and strongly urged her husband to reject any form of political reform. She had gone against the wishes of her grandmother, Queen Victoria, in refusing to marry the Duke of Clarence. She was a woman of obstinately strong character, and her determined and persistent friendship with the controversial monk Rasputin, much hated by the Russian people, was a factor in the monarchy's downfall.

THE WITNESS'S ACCOUNT

About midnight Yurovsky woke up the Tsar's family. I do not know if he told them the reason they had been awakened and where they were to be taken, but I positively affirm that it was Yurovsky who entered the room occupied by the Tsar's family. In about an hour the whole of the family, the doctor, the maid and the waiters got up, washed and dressed themselves.

....

"The blood was running in streams"

....

Just before Yurovsky went to awaken the family, two members of the Extraordinary Commission [of the Ekaterinburg Soviet] arrived at Ipatiev's house. Shortly after one o'clock am, the Tsar, the Tsaritsa, their four daughters, the maid, the doctor, the cook and the valets left their rooms. The Tsar carried the heir in his arms. The Emperor and the heir were dressed in gimnasterkas [soldiers' shirts] and wore caps. The Empress, her daughters and the others followed him. Yurovsky, his assistant and the two above-mentioned members of the Extraordinary Commission accompanied them. I was also present.

During my presence none of the Tsar's family asked any questions. They did not weep or cry. Having descended the stairs to the first floor, we went out into the court, and from there to the second door (counting from the gate) we entered the ground floor of the house. When the room (which adjoins the store room with a sealed door) was reached, Yurovsky ordered chairs to be brought, and his assistant brought three chairs. One chair was given to the Emperor, one to the Empress, and the third to the heir.

The Empress sat by the wall by the window, near the black pillar of the arch. Behind her stood three of her daughters (I knew their faces very well, because I had seen them every day when they walked in the garden, but I didn't know their names). The heir and the Emperor sat side by side almost in the middle of the room. Doctor Botkin stood behind the heir. The maid [Anna Demidova], a very tall woman, stood at the left of the door leading to the store room; by her side stood one of the Tsar's daughters (the fourth [Anastasia]). Two servants stood against the wall on the left from the entrance of the room.

The maid carried a pillow. The Tsar's daughters also brought small pillows with them. One pillow was put on the Empress's chair; another on the heir's chair. It seemed as if all of them guessed their fate, but not one of them uttered a single sound. At this moment eleven men entered the room: Yurovsky, his assistant, two members of the Extraordinary Commission, and seven Letts[2].

Yurovsky ordered me to leave, saying, 'Go on to the street, see if there is anybody there, and wait to see whether the shots have been heard.' I went out to the court, which was enclosed by a fence, but before I got to the street I heard the firing. I returned to the house immediately (only two or three minutes having elapsed) and upon entering the room where the execution had taken place, I saw that all the members of the Tsar's family were lying on the floor with many wounds in their bodies. The blood was running in streams. The doctor, the maid and two waiters had also been shot. When I entered the heir was still alive and moaned a little. Yurovsky went up and fired

2 – Possibly members of the Cheka (the Secret Police) or Austro-German prisoners-of-war. Either way, they were hired killers.

two or three more times at him. Then the heir was still.[3]

3 – Yurovsky had a little compassion. The day before the execution he had little Leonid Sedniev, the Tsar's kitchen boy, moved to the house next door. For some reason he decided to save his life.

DISCOVERING TUTANKHAMUN'S TOMB

---

*At first I could see nothing…
but presently, as my eyes grew
accustomed to the light, details of
the room within emerged slowly
from the mist*

WITNESSED BY
HOWARD CARTER

George Herbert, Earl of Carnarvon, was a wealthy English aristocrat who funded years of painstaking searching in the Valley of the Kings in Egypt – years in which nothing significant had been found. Carnarvon (1866-1923) was rich, but inflation began to take its toll and he warned his excavator, the archaeologist Howard Carter, that the 1922 season would have to be the last.

On 22 November 1922, Carter finally located and uncovered a hitherto untouched royal burial. Carter's discovery has sometimes been presented as simply lucky, but he had planned over a four-year period to find Tutankhamun's tomb. He could not have known that all its grave-goods would still be stacked inside it, but it was that particular tomb that he set out to discover. It was hidden under the excavation debris from three other tombs immediately above it: the tombs of Amenmesses, Ramesses III and Ramesses IV.

The discovery caused a sensation. Newspapers and magazines were full of pictures and descriptions.

The ancient objects that were brought out had a major effect on art and architecture in the 1920s. Suddenly bursting out of obscurity, 'King Tut' became the best-known pharaoh of them all.

THE WITNESS

Howard Carter (1874-1939) was an English Egyptologist who had worked as a draughtsman for Sir Flinders Petrie. He had a hunch that Tutankhamun's tomb was in the Valley of the Kings even though most other archaeologists believed that all the royal tombs in the Valley had been found. After years of systematic searching, his Egyptian workmen uncovered the steps leading down to the tomb.

Carter pretended that this was the moment of discovery, but he had peeped into the antechamber in mid-November, before Carnarvon arrived. It is also likely that Carter, Lord Carnarvon and Lady Evelyn Herbert went on, that night late in November, right through all the doors. Photographs show the pile of reeds and baskets Carter used to conceal one of the floor-level holes he had made for them to wriggle through. Officially, Carter did not break through the fourth sealed door until nearly three months later (16 February 1923), but the evidence is that their excitement got the better of them on that first night – when they saw all of the 'wonderful things' at once.

Carter was not an entirely truthful witness.

What was found in Tutankhamun's tomb?

By far the most iconic artefact found by Howard Carter inside the tomb of Tutankhamun was the young king's death mask, a stunning example of ancient goldsmith's art. The mask itself is made of solid gold inlaid with lapis lazuli, cornelian, quartz, obsidian, turquoise and coloured glass. It was found in the king's innermost tomb and stands 54cm (21in) high. The emblems on the front of the mask, the vulture (Nekhbet) and the cobra (Wadjet), were both included in order to offer the king protection in the afterlife. In Egyptian culture the vulture was considered to be a remarkably resourceful and intelligent bird, who used rocks as tools to gain entry and eat birds' eggs. The Cobra, or Asp, was a symbol of protection. It was expected to spit fire at the king's enemies if they approached his resting place.

THE WITNESS SETS THE SCENE

Slowly, desperately slowly it seemed to us as we watched, the remains of passage debris that encumbered the lower part of the doorway were removed, until at last we had the whole door clear before us. The decisive moment had arrived. With trembling hands I made a tiny breach in the upper left hand corner. Darkness and blank space, as far as an iron testing-rod could reach, showed that whatever lay beyond was empty, and not filled like the passage we had just cleared. Candle tests were applied as a precaution against possible foul gases, and then, widening the hole a little, I inserted the candle and peered in, Lord Carnarvon, Lady Evelyn [Lord Carnarvon's daughter] and Callender [an assistant] standing anxiously beside me to hear the verdict.

Character Profiles

Howard Carter

Howard Carter was a boy when he first became fascinated by ancient Egyptian civilization, and he was only 17 years old when he made his first visit to Alexandria, Egypt with Lady Amherst, a friend of the Carter family. Howard Carter was born in 1874, the son of a portrait artist, Samuel John Carter. His father taught him how to paint and draw accurately, and so his first job with the Egyptian

Exploration fund was as a tracer – someone who helps to copy drawings and hieroglyphs in order that they can be deciphered at a later date. Carter's first assignment came at Bani Hassan, when he was employed to help record and copy scenes from the walls of the tombs of the Princes of Middle Egypt. Apparently he worked extremely hard, and even slept in the tombs at night with only the bats for company, but it was under the guidance of William Flinders Petrie that Carter really grew as an archaeologist. When he finally discovered Tutankhamun's gold-laden tomb, it was at the end of an extremely long search.

Lord Carnarvon

George Herbert, the 5th Earl of Carnarvon, was born in 1866 at Highclere Castle near Newbury, England. Unlike his friend, Howard Carter, he was not gripped by Egyptology as a child, but preferred cars and horses. In fact, he described himself as a 'careful automobilist', but careful he certainly wasn't. He was given to speeding, and was involved in a major car accident which seriously weakened his health and made the damp, cold English winter climate intolerable. As a result he began to winter abroad, first visiting Cairo, Egypt in 1903. Lord Carnarvon was not simply a silent financial partner to Howard Carter, his political clout was necessary in order to make the research possible. Lord Carnarvon accumulated the largest collection of Egyptian artefacts in private ownership, and he sponsored the discovery of a total of six tombs in the Valley of the Kings at Luxor.

Tutankhamun

Today Tutankhamun, 'the living image of Amun', is the most famous of all the Egyptian pharaohs, though he was a short-lived and fairly insignificant ruler. He may be the 'King

Rathotis' mentioned by the ancient historian Manetho. It was Howard Carter's discovery of his tomb, and the incredible artefacts inside it, that lifted him out of obscurity and sparked a Western obsession with the Egyptian child-king. Tutankhamun lived over 3,300 years ago, during the period known as The New Kingdom, an era in which Egyptians worshipped one god – Aten, the sun god. The heart of the new kingdom was not the traditional Egyptian capital, Thebes, but a new city to the north, Akhetaten – meaning horizon of Aten. Tutankhamun was the son of Akhenaten and his second wife Kiya. He became king at the age of about nine, and married his half sister: Ankhesenpaaten, who was slightly older than him. It is unlikely that Tutankhamun would have made many important decisions during the early part of his reign. Instead they would have been made by high-ranking officials. The boy-king died, perhaps in battle or a chariot accident, at the age of about 18 and it was an official whose name was Ay, who arranged his burial. The arrangements lasted a total of 70 days.

THE WITNESS'S ACCOUNT

At first I could see nothing, the hot air escaping from the chamber causing the candle flame to flicker, but presently, as my eyes grew accustomed to the light, details of the room within emerged slowly from the mist, strange animals, statues, and gold - everywhere the glint of gold. For the moment - an eternity it must have seemed to the others standing by - I was struck dumb with amazement, and when Lord Carnarvon, unable to stand the suspense any longer, inquired anxiously, 'Can you see anything?' it was all I could do to get out the words, 'Yes, wonderful things.' Then widening the hole a little further, so that we both could see, we inserted an electric torch[1]...

1 – Carter was in effect dramatically re-enacting his earlier discovery of the ante-chamber for his patron's benefit.

My first care was to locate the wooden lintel above the [the fourth sealed] door: then very carefully I chipped away the plaster and picked out the small stones which formed the uppermost layer of the filling. The temptation to stop and peer inside at every moment was irresistible, and when, after about ten minutes' work, I had made a hole large enough to enable me to do so, I inserted an electric torch. An astonishing sight its light revealed, for there, within a yard of the doorway, stretching as far as one could see and blocking the entrance to the chamber, stood what to all appearances was a solid wall of gold. For the moment there was no clue as to its meaning, so as quickly as I dared I set to work to widen the hole.

With the removal of a very few stones the mystery of the golden wall was solved. We were at the entrance of the actual burial-chamber of the king, and that which barred our way was the side of an immense gilt shrine built to cover and protect the sarcophagus. It was visible now from the antechamber by the light of the standard lamps, and as stone after stone was removed, and its gilded surface came gradually into view, we could, as though by electric current, feel the tingle of excitement which thrilled the spectators behind the barrier.

....

"From top to bottom it was overlaid with gold"

....

It was, beyond any question, the sepulchral chamber in which we stood, for there, towering above us, was one of the great gilt shrines beneath which kings were laid. So enormous was this structure (17 feet by 11 feet, and 9 feet high, we found afterwards) that it filled within a little the entire area of the chamber, a space of some two feet only separating it from the walls on all four sides, while its roof, with cornice top and torus[2] moulding, reached almost to the ceiling. From

2 – A large semi-circular moulding.

top to bottom it was overlaid with gold, and upon its sides there were inlaid panels of brilliant blue faience, in which were represented, repeated over and over, the magic symbols which would ensure its strength and safety.

Around the shrine, resting upon the ground, there were a number of funerary emblems, and, at the north end, the seven magic oars the king would need to ferry himself across the waters of the underworld. The walls of the chamber, unlike those of the antechamber, were decorated with brightly painted scenes and inscriptions, brilliant in their colours, but evidently somewhat hastily executed.

THE BOMBING OF GUERNICA

*A Government official burst in
crying: "Guernica is destroyed.
The Germans bombed and
bombed and bombed."*

WITNESSED BY
NOEL MONKS
LUIS IRIONDO
AND JOSEFINA ODRIOZOLA

The Spanish Civil War that broke out in 1936 attracted the participation of forces beyond the borders of Spain, foreshadowing the alliances that would shortly afterwards break into open and large-scale conflict in World War II. Fascist régimes in Germany and Italy supported General Franco, while the Soviet Union backed the Republicans.

German bombers appeared in the skies over the town of Guernica in the late afternoon of 26 April, 1937 and attacked it without warning or provocation. Guernica was completely destroyed with an estimated loss of 1,650 lives. The sleepy Spanish town was transformed into a symbol of the atrocity of war. For the Germans, it was an experiment to find out how easy it would be to bomb a city into oblivion.

THE WITNESSES

1) Noel Monks was a correspondent covering the Spanish Civil War for the London newspaper

Daily Express. He was the first reporter to arrive on the scene immediately after the bombing.

2) Luis Iriondo was a 14-year-old boy living in Guernica. When the planes appeared, Luis ran across Guernica's main square and took refuge in a cellar. It was completely dark and there was no ventilation: after five minutes he could hardly breathe.

3) Josefina Odriozola was a girl of 14, shopping in the market with her mother, when the German planes closed in on the town. She spoke about it 70 years afterwards, still angry about the denials and the lies that followed the raid.

THE WITNESSES' ACCOUNTS

1) Noel Monks

We were about eighteen miles east of Guernica when Anton pulled to the side of the road, jammed on the brakes and started shouting. He pointed wildly ahead, and my heart shot into my mouth when I looked. Over the top of some small hills appeared a flock of planes. A dozen or so bombers were flying high. But down much lower, seeming just to skim the treetops were six Heinkel 52 fighters. The bombers flew on towards Guernica but the Heinkels, out for random plunder, spotted our car, and, wheeling like a flock of homing pigeons, they lined up the road - and our car.

Anton and I flung ourselves into a bomb hole, twenty yards to the side of the road. It was half filled with water, and we sprawled in the mud. We half knelt, half stood, with our heads buried in the muddy side of the crater.

After one good look at the Heinkels, I didn't look up again until they had gone. That seemed hours later, but it was probably less than twenty minutes. The planes made several runs along the road. Machine-gun bullets plopped into the mud ahead, behind, all around us. I began to shiver from sheer fright. Only the day before Steer, an old hand now, had briefed me about being strafed. 'Lie still and as flat as you can. But don't get up and start running, or you'll be bowled over for certain.'

When the Heinkels departed, out of ammunition I presumed, Anton and I ran back to our car. Nearby a military car was burning fiercely. All we could do was drag two riddled bodies to the side of the road. I was trembling all over now, in the grip of the first real fear I'd ever experienced.

Monks and his fellow reporters drove on, passing Guernica where they heard what they thought might be bombing. They went on to Balboa, where Monks joined his colleagues for dinner, which was interrupted by the news from Guernica.

A Government official, tears streaming down his face, burst into the dismal dining-room crying: 'Guernica is destroyed. The Germans bombed and bombed and bombed.' The time was about 9.30 pm. Captain Roberts banged a huge fist on the table and said: 'Bloody swine.'

Five minutes later I was in one of Mendiguren's limousines speeding towards Guernica. We were still a good ten miles away when I saw the reflection of Guernica's flames in the sky. As we drew nearer, on both sides of the road, men, women and children were sitting, dazed. I saw a priest in one group. I stopped the car and went up to him. 'What happened, Father?' I asked. His face was blackened, his clothes in tatters. He couldn't talk. He just pointed to the flames, still about four miles away, then whispered: 'Aviones… bombas… mucho, mucho.'

I was the first correspondent to reach Guernica, and was immediately pressed into service by some Basque soldiers collecting charred bodies that the flames had passed over. Some of the soldiers were sobbing like children. There were flames and smoke and grit, and the smell of burning human flesh was nauseating. Houses were collapsing into the inferno.

In the Plaza, almost surrounded by a wall of

fire, were about a hundred refugees. They were wailing and weeping and rocking to and fro. One middle-aged man spoke English. He told me: 'At four, before the market closed, many aeroplanes came. They dropped bombs. Some came low and shot bullets into the streets. Father Aroriategui was wonderful. He prayed with the people in the Plaza while the bombs fell.'

The only things left standing were a church, a sacred Tree, symbol of the Basque people, and, just outside the town, a small munitions factory. There hadn't been a single anti-aircraft gun in the town. It had been mainly a fire raid.

A sight that haunted me for weeks was the charred bodies of several women and children huddled together in what had been the cellar of a house. It had been a refugio.

2) Luis Iriondo

This bombardment lasted for three, maybe three and a half hours. You could hear the bombs and feel the hot currents of air being forced away by the explosions. I tried to pray. Finally it finished, and I didn't really know what had happened, I knew that it was a bombardment and expected houses to be in ruins. But when I left the shelter I could see that everything was on fire.

3) Josefina Odriozola

I remember it well. We left everything in the market and went home. We lived just outside the town, but the bombing started and we were there in the main square. Three planes flew in full of bombs and then left empty. Bomb, bomb, bomb, bomb, until everything was burning.

They burnt the city down with their planes and they denied they had done it - they blamed it on the Communists [when it had been the Fascists].

My sister was thirteen years older than me and they told her that the Reds had destroyed Guernica. But she said: 'No, the Reds don't have planes.' And they said to her: 'You little Red, we're going cut all your hair off.' Why? Because she was telling the truth. We couldn't even say the truth about the attack.

THE BATTLE OF BRITAIN

The sky seemed full of them, packed in layers thousands of feet deep

WITNESSED BY
PILOT OFFICER JOHN BEARD

The German Blitzkrieg technique (a massive air strike followed immediately by large-scale land invasion by tanks) had worked well on the mainland of Europe. The invasion of Britain would be harder, simply because the English Channel obstructed the tanks. Germany attempted to break British air power in the Battle of Britain in 1940, preparing the way for an invasion by sea. The Germans started their air attacks early in the summer. The British Royal Air Force was small, its pilots outnumbered by German pilots by four to one.

Fortunately, Hitler was distracted by his determination to defeat Russia, but the British victory in the Battle of Britain was nonetheless surprising.

The incident describes a typical German air attack up the Thames Estuary, heading towards London. A group of British pilots took off, climbed to 15,000 feet and waited for the German bomber planes to appear.

THE WITNESS

In the summer of 1940, Pilot Officer John Beard was twenty-one years old. He was a member of a squadron of Hurricanes based at an airfield near London.

THE WITNESS SETS THE SCENE

Minutes went by. Green fields and roads were now beneath us. I scanned the sky and the horizon for the first glimpse of the Germans. A new vector came through on the R.T. [radio telephone] and we swung round with the sun behind us. Swift on the heels of this I heard Yellow flight leader call through the earphones. I looked quickly toward Yellow's position - and there they were!

It was really a terrific sight and quite beautiful. First they seemed just a cloud of light as the sun caught the many glistening chromium parts of their engines, their windshields, and the spin of their airscrew discs. Then, as our squadron hurtled nearer, the details stood out. I could see the bright-yellow noses of Messerschmitt fighters sandwiching the bombers, and could even pick out some of the types. The sky seemed full of them, packed in layers thousands of feet deep. They came on steadily, wavering up and down along the horizon.

Character Profile

John Maurice Bentley Beard, AFC, DFM, was a member of No 249, Gold Coast Squadron. The Squadron's motto was *Pugnis et Calcibu*, which translates as 'With Fists and Heels'. It was formed in August 1918, from numbers 400, 401, 419 and 450 flights from Dundee. Squadron no 259's seaplanes provided anti-submarine patrols along the East coast of Scotland. It was disbanded in October 1919, but was reformed as a fighter unit in May 1940 at Church Fenton. At first, they were equipped with Spitfires, but after a month they switched to flying Hurricanes instead. In June 1940, one of its commanders, Flight Lieutenant J B Nicholson, became the only Fighter Command Pilot to receive a Victoria Cross during World War II, because he continued to attack and destroy an enemy plane even though his own aircraft was on fire. He suffered from severe burns following the incident but he proved that fighters from the Gold Coast Squadron consistently live up to their motto – they fight with everything they've got, with tooth and nail, with fists and heels.

THE WITNESS'S ACCOUNT

'Oh, golly,' I thought, 'golly, golly …'

And then any tension I had felt on the way suddenly left me. I was elated but very calm. I leaned over and switched on my reflector sight, flicked the catch on the gun button from 'Safe' to 'Fire', and lowered my seat till the circle and dot on the reflector sight shone darkly red in front of my eyes.

The squadron leader's voice came through the earphones, giving tactical orders. We swung round in a great circle to attack on their beam - into the thick of them. Then, on the order, down we went. I took my hand from the throttle lever so as to get both hands on the stick, and my thumb played neatly across the gun button. You have to steady a fighter just as you have to steady a rifle before you fire it.

My Merlin [the plane's engine] screamed as I went down in a steeply banked dive on to the tail of a forward line of Heinkels. I knew the air was full of aircraft flinging themselves about in all directions, but, hunched and snuggled down behind my sight, I was conscious only of the Heinkel I had picked out. As the angle of my dive increased, the enemy machine loomed larger in the sight field, heaved toward the red dot, and then he was there!

I had an instant's flash of amazement at the Heinkel proceeding so regularly on its way with a fighter on its tail. 'Why doesn't the fool move?' I thought, and actually caught myself flexing my muscles into the action I would have taken had I been he.

When he was square across the sight I pressed the button. There was a smooth trembling of my Hurricane as the eight-gun squirt shot out. I gave him a two-second burst and then another. Cordite fumes blew back into the cockpit, making an acrid mixture with the smell of hot oil and the air-compressors.

I saw my first burst go in and, just as I was on top of him and turning away, I noticed a red glow inside the bomber. I turned tightly into position again and now saw several short tongues of flame lick out along the fuselage. Then he went down in a spin, blanketed with smoke and with pieces flying off.

I left him plummeting down and, horsing back on my stick, climbed up again for more. The sky was clearing, but ahead toward London I saw a small, tight formation of bombers completely encircled by a ring of Messerschmitts. They were still heading north. As I raced forward, three flights of Spitfires came zooming up from beneath them in a sort of Prince-of-Wales's-feathers manoeuvre. They burst through upward and outward, their guns going all the time. They must have each got one, for an instant later I saw the most extraordinary sight of eight German bombers and fighters diving earthwards together in flames.

I turned away again and streaked after some distant specks ahead. Diving down, I noticed that the running progress of the battle had brought me over London again. I could see the network of streets with the green space of Kensington Gardens, and I had an instant's glimpse of the Round Pond, where I sailed boats when I was a child. In that moment, and as I was rapidly overhauling the Germans ahead, a Dornier 17 sped right across my line of flight, closely pursued by a Hurricane. And behind the Hurricane came two Messerschmitts. He was too intent to have seen them and they had not seen me! They were coming slightly toward me. It was perfect. A kick at the rudder and I swung in toward them, thumbed the gun button, and let them have it. The first burst was placed just the right distance ahead of the leading Messerschmitt. He ran slap into it and he simply came to pieces in the air. His companion, with one of the speediest and most brilliant 'get-outs' I have ever seen, went right away in a half Immelmann turn.[1] I missed him completely. He must almost have been hit by the pieces of the leader but he got away. I hand it to him.

At that moment some instinct made me glance up at my rear-view mirror and spot two Messerschmitts closing in on my tail. Instantly I hauled back on the stick and streaked upward. And just in time. For as I flicked into the climb,

1 – The Immelmann turn (climb, loop, then return) was a popular aerobatic manoeuvre in World War I, still sometimes used in World War II.

I saw the tracer streaks pass beneath me. As I turned I had a quick look round the 'office' [cockpit]. My fuel reserve was running out and I had only about a second's supply of ammunition left. I was certainly in no condition to take on two Messerschmitts. But they seemed no more eager than I was. Perhaps they were in the same position, for they turned away for home. I put my nose down and did likewise.

The Hawker Hurricane

Sydney Camm, an aircraft designer for Hawker Aircraft Ltd, began working on the Hawker Hurricane fighter plane in 1934, inspired by the fact that the Air Ministry was looking for a new fighter plane built around the new Rolls Royce 'Merlin' engine. Camm's design evolved through several adaptations but was ultimately destined to revolutionize the way fighter planes were built. The Hawker Hurricane was the first fighter monoplane to join the Royal Air Force and the first British combat aircraft capable of exceeding 300 mph in level flight. It formed a legendary partnership with the Supermarine Spitfire in Britain's defence during the Battle of Britain. Often underrated in favour of the Spitfire, the Hurricane was more rugged and versatile and equipped more than three-fifths of RAF's Fighter Command Squadrons. The Hurricane was also designed with economy in mind, which was a very wise move, because come the advent of WWII, economy became more important than ever to the Ministry of Defence. In August 1935, following a series of vigorous tests, production began on the first prototype Hurricane: K5083, incorporating the Rolls Royce P12 Merlin engine. The completed sections were taken to Hawker's assembly shed in Brooklands, and assembled there on 23 October 1935. Ground testing and taxi trials took place over the next two weeks, and by 6 November 1935, she was finally ready to fly. Between them, the Hurricane and the Spitfire enabled the British to win the Battle of Britain, when compared to the German equivalent, the Messerschmitt, which was more powerful and carried more guns, the British planes were lighter, more manoeuvrable and the British pilots better trained.

PEARL HARBOR

A terrible explosion caused the ship to shake violently. I looked at the boat deck and everything seemed aflame forward of the mainmast

WITNESSED BY
MARINE CORPORAL E. C. NIGHTINGALE
AND COMMANDER MITSUO FUCHIDA

The Japanese air attack on the American fleet at Pearl Harbor on 7 December 1941 came as a complete surprise. The first wave of planes arrived at 7.53 am. By midday, the carriers that had launched the planes were preparing to return to Japan, leaving 2,403 people dead, 188 planes destroyed and eight battleships seriously damaged or destroyed. This unprovoked attack of undeclared war made America's entry into World War II certain.

THE WITNESSES

1) Marine Corporal E. C. Nightingale was a member of the crew of the battleship *USS Arizona*. Ten minutes into the attack, a bomb plunged through the ship's two armoured decks and hit its magazine. The huge explosion engulfed the ship in flames, and sank it within a few minutes. 1,300 people were killed.

2) Commander Mitsuo Fuchida led the first wave of the air attack and published his recollections in 1951.

THE WITNESSES' ACCOUNTS

1) Marine Corporal E. C. Nightingale

At approximately eight o'clock on the morning of December 7, 1941, I was leaving the breakfast table when the ship's siren for air defence sounded. Suddenly I heard an explosion. I ran to the port door leading to the quarterdeck and saw a bomb strike a barge of some sort alongside the *Nevada*. I believe at this point our anti-aircraft battery opened up.

We stood around awaiting orders. General Quarters sounded and I started for my battle station. I was about three-quarters of the way to the first platform on the mast when it seemed as though a bomb struck our quarterdeck. I could hear fragments whistling past me. As soon as I reached the first platform, I saw Second Lieutenant Simonson lying on his back with blood on his shirt front. I bent over him and taking him by the shoulders asked if there was anything I could do. He was dead, or so nearly so that speech was impossible. Seeing there was nothing I could do for the Lieutenant, I continued to my battle station.

I reported to Major Shapley that Mr Simonson had been hit and there was nothing to be done for him. There was a lot of talking going on and I shouted for silence which came immediately. [Then] a terrible explosion caused the ship to shake violently. I looked at the boat deck and everything seemed aflame forward of the mainmast. The Major ordered us to leave.

I followed the Major down the port side of the tripod mast. The railings, as we ascended, were very hot and as we reached the boat deck I noted that it was torn up and burned. The bodies of the dead were thick, and badly burned men were heading for the quarterdeck, only to fall apparently dead or badly wounded. The Major and I went between No. 3 and No. 4 turret to the starboard side and found Lieutenant Commander Fuqua ordering the men over the side and assisting the wounded. He seemed exceptionally calm and the Major stopped and they talked for a moment. Charred bodies were everywhere. I made my way to the quay and started to remove my shoes when I suddenly found myself in the water.

I think the concussion of a bomb threw me in. I started swimming for the pipe line which was about one hundred and fifty feet away. I was about half way when my strength gave out. My clothes and shocked condition sapped my strength, and I was about to go under when Major Shapley [saw] my distress, grasped my shirt and told me to hang onto his shoulders while he swam in. I would have drowned but for the Major. We finally reached the beach where a marine directed us to a bomb shelter, where I was given dry clothes and a place to rest.

2) Commander Mitsuo Fuchida

It was 0749 when I ordered my radioman to send the command, 'Attack!'

Leading the whole group, Lieutenant Commander Murata's torpedo bombers headed downward to launch their torpedoes, while Lieutenant Commander Itayay's fighters raced forward to sweep enemy fighters from the air. Takahashi's dive-bomber group had climbed for altitude and was out of sight. My bombers, meanwhile, made a circuit toward Barbers Point. No enemy fighters were in the air, nor were there any gun flashes from the ground. The effectiveness of our attack was now certain, and a message, 'Surprise attack successful!' was accordingly sent to *Akagi* [the Japanese flagship].

The attack was opened with the first bomb falling on Wheeler Field, followed shortly by dive-bombing attacks upon Hickam Field and the bases at Ford Island. Lieutenant Commander Itaya's fighters had full command of the air over Pearl Harbour. About four enemy fighters which took off were promptly shot down. By 0800 there were no enemy planes in the air, and our fighters began strafing the airfields.

As we closed in, enemy anti-aircraft fire began to concentrate on us. Dark gray puffs burst all around. Most of them came from ships' batteries, but land batteries were also active. Suddenly my plane bounced as if struck by a club. When I looked back to see what had happened, the radioman said: 'The fuselage is holed and the rudder wire damaged.' We were fortunate that the plane was still under control. I concentrated my attention on the lead plane to note the instant his bomb was dropped. Suddenly a cloud came between the bombsight and the target, and just as I was thinking that we had already overshot, the lead plane banked slightly and turned right toward Honolulu. We had missed the release point because of the cloud and would have to try again.

My group circled for another attempt. We were about to begin our second bombing run when there was a colossal explosion in battleship row. A huge column of dark red smoke rose to 1000 metres. It must have been the explosion of a ship's [the *Arizona*'s] powder magazine. The shock wave was felt even in my plane, several miles away from the harbour.

We began our run. This time the lead bomber was successful. I immediately lay flat on the cockpit floor and slid open a peephole cover in order observe the fall of the bombs. I watched four bombs plummet toward the earth. The target - two battleships moored side by side - lay ahead. The bombs became smaller and smaller and finally disappeared. I held my breath until two tiny puffs of smoke flashed suddenly on the ship to the left, and I shouted, 'Two hits!' When an armour-piercing bomb with a time fuse hits the target, the result is almost unnoticeable from a great altitude. I presumed that it was battleship *Maryland* we had hit.

The bombers headed north to return to the carriers. Pearl Harbor and the air bases had been pretty well wrecked by the fierce strafings and bombings. The imposing naval array of an hour before was gone.

THE ALLIED LANDINGS IN NORMANDY

We're deafened by the aeroplanes, which make a never–ending sound

WITNESSED BY
MARIE-LOUISE OSMONT

In the early hours of 6 June 1944, American and British paratroopers were dropped behind the invasion beaches in order to disrupt the German communications. Then at dawn the invasion by sea began. An armada of vessels landed thousands of troops at five selected beaches along the Normandy coast. The landings were successful, though not easily won, and the final defeat of Nazi Germany had begun.

THE WITNESS

Marie-Louise Osmont lived with her husband, a doctor, in the Chateau Périers, overlooking Sword Beach. When the Germans occupied France they commandeered their house, but allowed the Osmonts to stay on in a few rooms. On the night of 5-6 June 1944 she was woken up by the sound of planes and gunfire. She was uncertain whether they were German or Allied. Marie-Louis kept this diary account.

THE WITNESS'S ACCOUNT

Little by little the grey dawn comes up, but this time around, from the intensity of the aircraft and the cannon, an idea springs to mind: landing! I get dressed hurriedly. I cross the garden, the men recognize me. In one of the foxholes in front of the house, I recognize one of the young men from the office; he has headphones on his ears, the telephone being removed there.

Airplanes, cannon right on the coast, almost on us. I cross the road, run to the farm, come across Meltemps.

'Well?' I say, 'Is this it, this time?'

'Yes,' he says, 'I think so, and I'm really afraid we're in a sector that's being attacked; that's going to be something!'

We're deafened by the aeroplanes, which make a never-ending sound, very low; obviously what I thought were German aeroplanes are quite simply English ones, protecting the landing.

Coming from the sea, a dense artificial cloud; it's ominous and begins to be alarming; the first hiss over our heads. I feel cold; I'm agitated. I go home, dress more warmly, close the doors; I go to fetch Bernice [a neighbour] to get into the trench, a quick bowl of milk, and we run - just in time! The shells hiss and explode continually.

In the trench in the farmyard (the one that was dug in 1940) we find three or four Germans: Leo the cook, his helper, and two others, crouching, not proud except for Leo, who stays outside to watch. We ask them, 'Tommy come?' They say 'yes', with conviction. Morning in the trench, with overhead the hisses and whines that make you bend even lower. For fun Leo fires a rifle shot at a low-flying airplane, but the Spiess ['Sarge', the German Sergeant-Major] appears and tells him off horribly; this is not the time to attract attention.

Shells are exploding everywhere, and not far away, with short moments of calm; we take advantage of these to run and deal with the animals, and we return with hearts pounding to burrow into the trench. Each time a shell hisses by too low, I cling to the back of the cook's helper, it makes me feel a little more secure, and he turns around with a vague smile. The fact is that we're all afraid.

Around noon there was a bit of a lull. We leave to try to have lunch; I busy myself with the fire, Bernice with the soup and potatoes; it's cooking. We start to seat ourselves around the table, two mouthfuls of soup, and then everything changes with tremendous speed. Someone - a Frenchman on the road, the soldiers at the gate - someone says: 'The Tommies!' We watch the soldiers. They hide on both sides of the gate, watching in the distance in panic, confusion painted on their faces. And suddenly we hear these words: 'The tanks!' A first burst of tracer bullets, very red, sweeps the gate; men crouch down. Bernice and I hide in a corner of the room. There's banging in every direction. We're going to have to go somewhere else. Standing in our corner, we gulp a plate of soup, while the Spiess, who has been shouting orders, comes revolver in hand to see whether men are hiding with us. Everything starts happening. Evidently, they're going to try to leave with their trucks. A German tank arrives and takes the Spiess away. The shells explode. The mean Spiess had guts. He came and went heedless of the shells, attended to everything – and he probably organized having the trucks leave; orders from higher up didn't seem to come.

Impossible to stay in this house at the edge of the road with such thin walls. We cut two slices of bread, the same amount of cold meat and, hugging the walls of the outbuildings, we make it to the trench.

Around six o'clock a lull. We get out and go toward the house to care for the animals. Then we see the first damage. Branches of the big walnut broken, roof on the outbuildings heavily damaged, a heap of broken roof tiles on the ground, a few windowpanes at my place -

hundreds of slates blown off the chateau, walls cracked - but at Bernice's it's worse. A shell has exploded in her kitchen, and the whole room is devastated. The dog Frick that I had shut up in the next room so he wouldn't get killed on the road, is all right and sleeping on a seat. But we realize that if we had stayed there, we would both have been killed. Bernice takes the disaster very well; we try to straighten up the unspeakable mess a little. Out of the question to eat the soup and mashed potatoes that have been prepared; everything is black with dust and full of shards of glass. Someone gives us soup from the farm. We talk with them for a short while and note the Germans haven't taken away all the trucks from the drive; there are also a lot of vehicles still in the park.

English tanks are silhouetted from time to time on the road above Périers. Impassioned exchanges on the road with the people from the farm; we are stupefied by the suddenness of events. I take a few steps down the drive, toward the Deveraux house, and suddenly I see the replacement Sarge and his comrade hugging the field wall. You feel that these two men are lost, disorientated, sad. Later, almost night, I see them again, their faces deliberately blackened with charcoal, crossing the park. What will be their fate? How many of them are still in the area, hiding and watching?

A VISIT TO A NAZI DEATH CAMP

Could the people in their death agony see the SS man's eye as he watched them?

WITNESSED BY
ALEXANDER WERTH

The Nazis set up the first concentration camp shortly after Hitler came to power in 1933. The camp system evolved to include about a hundred camps divided into two types. There were concentration camps which were to supply slave labour for nearby factories. There were also death camps for the systematic extermination of groups of people regarded by the Nazis as undesirable. These included Jews, gypsies, homosexuals and the mentally handicapped.

Towards the end of the Second World War, advancing Allied troops liberated the camps one-by-one, revealing for the first time to the outside world the full horror of the death camps. Here was the price of Nazism. The first of these liberations came in July 1944 when Soviet troops entered Maidanek, which was a Polish death camp about two miles from the city of Lublin.

Maidanek was set up by the Germans in 1941 after they took control of the Russian-occupied part of Poland. It was from the first a death camp. Most of the victims were trawled from the immediate neighbourhood, but Maidanek was also used to exterminate Jews arriving from Western Europe, including France and the Netherlands. Probably 1.5 million people were systematically murdered at Maidanek during just three years in action, 1941-44, an astonishing and horrifying number of victims.

THE WITNESS

Soviet troops entered Maidanek camp in July 1944. A week later, Soviet army officers organized a guided tour of the facility for a group of reporters, specifically to show the world the true nature of Nazi Germany. Alexander Werth (1901-1969) was a Russian-born naturalized British writer and journalist, acting as a correspondent for *The Sunday Times* and the BBC. He joined a group of fellow reporters in a tour of the camp accompanied by Soviet soldiers, and described it shortly after its capture. He was fluent in both Russian and English.

The BBC refused to broadcast Werth's report. His description of the camp was so grotesque and unbelievable that they assumed it was a piece of Soviet propaganda, on a level with World War I propaganda story about German soldiers bayoneting babies. But when British and American troops later captured camps on the Western Front, camps such as Dachau and Buchenwald, the BBC realized that Alexander Werth's report from Maidanek had been true.

THE WITNESS'S ACCOUNT

My first reaction to Maidanek was a feeling of surprise. I had imagined something horrible and sinister beyond words. It was nothing like that. It looked singularly harmless from outside. 'Is *that* it?' was my first reaction when we stopped at what looked like a large workers' settlement. Behind us was the many towered skyline of Lublin. There was much dust on the road, and the grass a dull, greenish-grey colour.

The camp was separated from the road by a couple of barbed-wire fences, but these did not look particularly sinister, and might have been put up outside any military or semi-military establishment. The place was large; like a whole town of barracks painted a pleasant soft green. There were many people around - soldiers and civilians. A Polish sentry opened the barbed-wire gate to let cars enter the central avenue, with large green barracks on either side. And we stopped outside a large barrack marked *Bad und Desinfektion II*.[1] 'This,' somebody said, 'is where large numbers of those arriving at the camp were brought in.'

The inside of this barrack was made of concrete, and water taps came out of the wall, and around the room there were benches where the clothes were put down and *afterwards* collected. So this was the place into which they were driven. Or perhaps they were politely invited to 'Step this way, please?' Did any of them suspect, while washing themselves after a long journey, what

1 – Bath and Disinfection.

would happen a few minutes later? Anyway, after the washing was over, they were asked to go into the next room; at this point even the most unsuspecting must have begun to wonder.

For the 'next room' was a series of large square concrete structures, each about one-quarter of the size of the bath-house, and, unlike it, had no windows. The naked people (men one time, women another time, children the next) were driven or forced from the bath-house into these dark concrete boxes - about five yards square - and then, with 200 or 250 people packed into each box - and it was completely dark there, except for a small light in the ceiling and the spyhole in the door - the process of gassing began.

First some hot air was pumped in from the ceiling and then the pretty pale-blue crystals of Zyklon[2] were showered down on the people, and in the hot wet air they rapidly evaporated. In anything from two to ten minutes everybody was dead. . . There were six concrete boxes - gas-chambers -

2 – Werth's report uses the spelling 'Cyclon', but 'Zyklon' is the usual spelling, and more precisely 'Zyklon-B'.

side by side. 'Nearly two thousand people could be disposed of here simultaneously,' one of the guides said.

But what thoughts passed through these people's minds during those first few minutes while the crystals were falling; could anyone still believe that this humiliating process of being packed into a box and standing there naked, rubbing backs with other naked people, had anything to do with disinfection?

At first it was all very hard to take in, without an effort of the imagination. There were a number of very dull-looking concrete structures which, if their doors had been wider, might anywhere else have been mistaken for a row of nice little garages. But the doors - the doors! They were heavy steel doors, and each had a heavy steel bolt. And in the middle of the door was a spyhole, a circle, three inches in diameter composed of about a hundred small holes. Could the people in their death agony see the SS man's eye as he watched them? Anyway, the SS man had nothing to fear: his eye was well protected by the steel netting over the spyhole.

Then a touch of blue on the floor caught my eye. It was very faint, but still legible. In blue chalk someone had scribbled the word *vergast* and had drawn crudely above it a skull and crossbones. I had never seen this word before but it obviously meant 'gassed' - and not merely 'gassed' but: with, that eloquent little prefix *ver*, 'gassed out'.[3] That's this job finished, and now for the next lot. The blue chalk came into motion when there was nothing but a heap of naked corpses inside.

But what cries, what curses, what prayers perhaps, had been uttered inside that gas chamber only a few minutes before?

3 – The word *vergast* does indeed mean 'gassed'. The word *gast* means 'guest' or 'visitor', so perhaps this is some grisly attempt at humour by the guards.

RAISING THE US FLAG OVER IWO JIMA

For the first time during World War Two, an American flag was flying above what was considered traditional Japanese territory

WITNESSED BY
SCOTT TANK, AMERICAN MARINE

The capture of the island of Iwo Jima was a highly significant moment in the Pacific War. The Americans had fought hard to capture one Pacific island after another from the Japanese, driving them back towards Japan. The aim was to destroy the Japanese Empire. But Iwo Jima was different. It was traditionally regarded as part of the Japanese homeland, and therefore equivalent to taking part of 'mainland' Japan. It marked a crucial stage in Japan's defeat. The fighting for Iwo Jima was very fierce.

Raising the American flag at the summit of Mt Suribachi during the battle for Iwo Jima has become one of the iconic moments of modern warfare. This is largely because of a remarkable and very powerful photograph of the flag as it was being raised. It is an image that looks as if it has been directed by a great film director intent on portraying US Marines as war heroes. In a way the photograph is misleading, in that the flag had already been raised on Mt Suribachi about two hours earlier and the famous iconic photograph shows the *second* raising of the flag.

The second flag-raising was not undertaken just for the sake of taking a memorable photograph. It was deemed necessary because the first flag, put up shortly after the Marines had gained the top of the mountain after hard fighting, was too small to be seen easily from the foot of the mountain; a second, larger flag was needed.

The first flag-raising was photographed, but the image is less striking than the much better-known photograph of the second flag-raising. The young soldiers who raised the second flag were Ira Hayes, Franklin Sousley, John Bradley, Harlon Block, Michael Strank and Rene Gagnon. The last two are not visible in the photograph because they are hidden behind the other four men. Sousley, Block and Strank died in battle shortly afterwards and the survivors did not want to be heroes. When Ira Hayes, a Pima Indian, was hailed as a national hero by President Truman he was mortified; 'How could I feel like a hero when only five men in my platoon of forty-five survived?' Bradley, the central figure in the famous photograph, died in 1994.

THE WITNESS

Scott Tank was one of the American soldiers who raised the first flag on the crest of the mountain. The last surviving member of that team was Corporal Charles W. Lindberg, a friend of Scott Tank's. Lindberg died at the age of 86 in 2007.

THE WITNESS'S ACCOUNT

It was the job of the 28th Regiment, 5th Division, to capture Mount Suribachi. They reached the base of the mountain on the afternoon of February 21, and by nightfall the next day the Marines had almost completely surrounded it.

As part of that Marine group, 24-year-old Corporal Charles Lindberg, a combat veteran of the Guadalcanal and the Bougainville campaign, watched the intense bombardment of Iwo Jima and realized that the landing at Red Beach One would be anything but easy. 'The Japs had the whole beach zeroed in. Most of the fire was coming from Suribachi,' he recalled. Surrounding Mount Suribachi were cliffs, tunnels, mines, booby traps, and ravines. The hostile terrain proved to be as tough an enemy as the Japanese who were firmly entrenched on the mountain.

At 8 am on February 23, a patrol of forty men from 3rd Platoon, E Company, 2nd Battalion, 28th Marines, led by Lieutenant Harold G. Schrier, assembled at the base of Mount Suribachi. The platoon's mission was to take the crater of Suribachis peak and raise the U.S. flag. As a member of the first combat patrol to scale Mount Suribachi, Corporal Lindberg took his 72-pound flamethrower and started the tortuous climb up the rough terrain to the top.

As they reached the top, the patrol members took positions around the crater watching for pockets of enemy resistance as other members of the patrol looked for something on which to raise the flag. Present at the crest were six Marines of a forty-man patrol. They were Lieutenant Schrier, Sergeant Thomas, Sergeant Hansen, Private First Class Charlo, Private First Class Michels, and Corporal Charles W. Lindberg.

At approximately 10.20 am, the flag was hoisted on a steel pipe above the island. The sight of the small American flag flying from atop Mount Suribachi thrilled men all over the island. And for the first time during World War II, an American flag was flying above what was considered traditional Japanese territory. This symbol of victory sent a wave of strength to the battle-weary fighting men below, and struck a further mental blow against the island's defenders.

Marine Corps photographer Sergeant Lou Lowery captured this first flag raising on film just as the enemy hurled a grenade in his direction. Dodging the grenade, Lowery hurled his body over the edge of the crater and tumbled 50 feet.

His camera lens was shattered, but he and his film were safe.

As Corporal Lindberg would later remark, 'Suribachi was easy to take; it was getting there that was so hard!' Of the forty-man patrol, thirty-six were killed or wounded in later fighting on Iwo Jima including Lindberg himself who would be shot through the stomach and arm a week later on 1 March, 1945. For his heroism Lindberg would receive the Purple Heart and Silver Star Medal with the citation reading in part:

Repeatedly exposing himself to hostile grenades and machine-gun fire in order that he might reach and neutralize enemy pill-boxes at the base of Mount Suribachi, Corporal Lindberg courageously approached within ten or fifteen yards of the emplacements before discharging his weapon, thereby assuring the annihilation of the enemy and the successful completion of this platoon's mission. While engaged in an attack on hostile cave positions on March 1, he fearlessly exposed himself to accurate enemy fire and was subsequently wounded and evacuated.

THE ASSASSINATION OF GANDHI

It was one of those shining Delhi evenings, not at all warm but alight with the promise of spring

WITNESSED BY
VINCENT SHEEAN

Gandhi worked long and hard to achieve independence for India. But with independence came something he totally opposed – the partitioning of the sub-continent in 1947 into two separate states – a mainly Muslim Pakistan and a mainly Hindu India. Gandhi did not take part in the celebration of independence. The violence that accompanied partition was something he abhorred.

The various political factions in India had quarrelled violently among themselves for decades. There were extremists who hated Gandhi. One was Nathuram Godse, who believed that it was Gandhi who was responsible for partition. He tried four times to assassinate Gandhi, and at the fifth attempt he succeeded.

In New Delhi in the early evening of 30 January, 1948 Gandhi was due to hold a prayer-meeting.

THE WITNESS

Vincent Sheean (1899-1975) was an American novelist and journalist. He visited and reported on a variety of trouble spots round the world during World War II and in the years immediately before and after it.

In 1947, Sheean travelled to India. There he became not just an observer but a follower of Gandhi. He hoped to find some meaning in the unusually violent events he had witnessed as a reporter.

THE WITNESS SETS THE SCENE

I got a taxi and went out to Birla House[1] in time for the prayer-meeting. This time I was alone. I stationed my taxi under a tree opposite the gate of Birla House and walked down the drive to the prayer-ground. It was not yet five o'clock and people were still streaming in on foot, in cars and with tongas. As I came on to the prayer-ground

1 – The house where Gandhi was then living, and opened to the public in 1973 as the Gandhi Smriti (Gandhi Memorial).

363

at the end of the garden I ran into Bob Stimson, the Delhi correspondent for the BBC. We fell into talk and I told him about the journey to Amritsar and what had taken place there. It was unusual to see any representatives of the press at the prayer-meeting; Bob explained that he had submitted some questions to the Mahatma for the BBC and thought he might as well stay for the prayers since he was on the premises. He looked at his watch and said: 'Well, this is strange. Gandhi's late. He's practically never late.'

We both looked at our watches again. It was 5.12 [pm] by my watch when Bob said: 'There he is.' We stood near the corner of the wall, on the side of the garden where he was coming, and watched the evening light fall on his shining dark-brown head.

Character Profiles

. . . .

Mahatma Gandhi

Mohandas Karamchand Gandhi was born in Pabander, India in 1869. His father was a high-ranking minister to the local ruler, and as a consequence Mohandas enjoyed a relatively privileged upbringing. He was married, at the age of 13, to a girl called Kasturba, who was even younger than him, and in 1888 he decided to attend university in England in order to become a lawyer, much to the disapproval of his elders. Gandhi was called to the bar in 1891, and returned to India later that year to practise law, before spending a considerable period of time in South Africa. It was here that Gandhi first encountered racism in its rawest sense, and saw how far Indians really were from being considered equal in the eyes of the world. His experiences there triggered a political awakening that saw Gandhi emerge as a leader of the Indian community, not only in South Africa, but eventually in the rest of the world. He has also become a hero for the pacifists all over the globe because he achieved so much change whilst maintaining a strictly non-violent stance.

....

Nathuram Godse

Nathuram Godse is still a controversial figure in Indian history because of the part he played in the assassination of Mahatma Gandhi. He was born in Baramati, India in 1910 to a post office worker, Vinayak Vamanrao Godse, and his wife Lakshmi Godse. He was educated at an English language school but dropped out to become an activist with the Hindu Mahasabha and the RSS, both Hindu nationalist organisations. During childhood, Gandhi had been a hero of Godse's, but he came to believe that Gandhi had betrayed Hindu interests in an effort to appease minority groups. He blamed Gandhi for his role in the partition of India into two separate states, Muslim Pakistan, and Hindu India.The partition left many thousands of people dead, many of whom Godse considered to be martyrs to the Hindu cause. He believed that Gandhi had to die for his part in the struggles. Sadly, the violence did not end with Gandhi's assassination. Despite the best efforts of Gandhi's loved ones, Godse was executed for his part in the killing on 15 November 1949.

....

Vincent Sheean

James Vincent Sheean was born to Irish American parents in Illinois in 1899. He left home at the age of 17 to enrol at the University of Chicago, where he became a reporter for the Daily Maroon. Three years into Vincent's study programme his mother died, and he was forced to leave university. He got a short-lived job at a local Chicago newspaper before heading to New York, where he worked for the Daily News, based in Manhattan. In New York Vincent spent much of his time drinking and carousing with radicals in the cafes and bars of Greenwich village, before heading overseas in search of adventure. During his career as a foreign correspondent Vincent Sheean met and became friends with some extraordinary individuals. Ernest Hemingway was one of his favourite drinking companions, and he witnessed the advance of Bolshevism in Russia. In short, Sheean had an uncanny habit of finding himself right at the heart of the action. He was accustomed to being in dangerous situations and had seen more than his fair share of bloodshed, but it was during the events of Gandhi's assassination that he ceased to be a journalist and experienced those horrifying moments as a sympathizer and follower rather than as a journalist. Perhaps this is what makes his account of that day so moving.

THE WITNESS'S ACCOUNT

It was one of those shining Delhi evenings, not at all warm but alight with the promise of spring. I felt well and happy and grateful to be here. Bob and I stood idly talking, I do not remember about what, and watching the Mahatma advance toward us over the grass, leaning lightly on two of 'the girls', with two or three other members of his 'family' (family or followers) behind them. I read afterward that he had sandals on his feet but I did not see them. To me it looked as if he walked barefoot on the grass. It was not a warm evening and he was wrapped in homespun shawls. He passed by us on the other side and turned to ascend the four or five brick steps which led to the terrace or prayer-ground.

Here, as usual, there was a clump of people, some of whom were standing and some of whom had gone on their knees or bent low before him. Bob and I turned to watch - we were perhaps ten feet away from the steps - but the clump of people cut off our view of the Mahatma now; he was so small. Then I heard four small, dull, dark explosions. 'What's that?' I said to Bob in sudden horror. 'I don't know,' he said. I remember that he grew pale in an instant. 'Not the Mahatma!' I said, and then I knew.

Inside my own head there occurred a wavelike disturbance which I can only compare to a storm at sea - wind and wave surging tremendously back and forth. I remember all this distinctly; I do not believe that I lost consciousness even for a moment, although there may have been an instant or two of half-consciousness. I recoiled upon the brick wall and leaned against it, bent almost in two. I felt the consciousness of the Mahatma leave me then - I know of no other way of expressing this: he left me. The storm inside my head continued for some little time - minutes, perhaps; I have no way of reckoning. . .

It was during this time, apparently, that many things happened: a whole external series of events took place in my immediate neighbourhood - a few yards away - and I was unaware of them. A doctor was found; the police took charge; the body of the Mahatma was carried away; the crowd melted, perhaps urged to do so by the police. I saw none of this. The last I saw of the Mahatma he was advancing over the grass in the evening light, approaching the steps. When I finally took my fingers out of my mouth and stood up, dry-eyed, there were police and soldiers and not many people, and there was Bob Stimson. He was rather breathless; he had gone somewhere to telephone to the BBC.

He came with me down the steps to the lawn, where we walked up and down beside the flower-bed for a while. The room with the glass doors and windows, by the rose garden at the end of the arbour, had a crowd of people around it. Many were weeping. The police were endeavouring to make them leave. Bob could not tell me anything except that the Mahatma had been taken inside that room. On the following day he told me that he had seen him carried away and that the khadi which he wore was heavily stained with blood.

The Partition of India

The Islamic republic of Pakistan was created on 14 August 1947. At midnight on the following day India won its independence from British colonial rule, ending 350 years of British presence there.

The British left India split into two parts on the basis of religion. The nation of Pakistan was set up as an Islamic state, and India was set up to be a secular, but mainly Hindu, state. Mahatma Gandhi helped to lead the Indian people in their struggle for independence from Britain, but there were several other nationalist movements at work in India during this time. The Indian National Congress wanted Britain to leave India, but the Muslim League called for partition as well. The British had followed a divide and rule policy in India. They tended to see the Indian population in terms of religion, and treated the different groups as if they were totally separate entities, rather than encouraging them to coexist peacefully. The Muslim Indians wanted their own Indian Islamic homeland within the sub continent, and they were prepared to fight to obtain it. At the same time there was a Hindu revivalist movement, of which Nathuram Godse was part, who resented the Muslims for their recent domination of India. They wanted to introduce new laws banning the slaughter of cattle, a sacred animal to Hindus but a cheap source of meat to Muslims. The Hindu nationalists also wanted to change the national script from Persian to Hindu Devanagri script, which would effectively have made Hindi a dominant language over Urdu. A violent power struggle erupted between Muslim segregationists and Hindu nationalists. Thousands of people died in the riots following partition. The violence persists today, with both Pakistan and India claiming sovereignty over the northern region of Kashmir.

THE CUBAN REVOLUTION

*Within seconds, a hail of bullets
– at least that's how it seemed to
us – descended on our group of
eighty-two men*

WITNESSED BY
CHE GUEVARA

The Cuban Revolution was a remarkable romantic adventure that ought not to have succeeded. The revolution was under-manned, under-funded, under-equipped and under-organized. A slow and leaky leisure yacht, the *Granma*, was secured by Fidel Castro for the trip from Mexico to Cuba, but she was seriously overladen.

Instead of arriving in Cuba to coincide with a rising in Santiago de Cuba, Castro's boat was two days late. By then Batista's troops had put down the Santiago rising and were free to deal with the little expeditionary landing force. The *Granma* was spotted by a helicopter, and the rebels were forced to beach her in a swamp. Most of the 82 revolutionaries who landed were killed or captured during 11 days of fighting. Only twelve survived to escape to the mountains, including Fidel and Raul Castro and Che Guevara. The Cuban Revolution started very badly. Surprisingly, it succeeded in the end.

THE WITNESS

Ernesto 'Che' Guevara was an Argentinian doctor who joined Fidel Castro in Mexico and became one of the leaders of the 1956-59 Cuban Revolution. Guevara was given high public office, but he found it impossible to toe a party line. After leaving Cuba in 1965, Che set up revolutionary guerrilla forces in the Congo and Bolivia, where he was captured and killed two years later by Bolivian government troops.

Che was a charismatic revolutionary leader. The nickname 'Che' is Argentinian-Spanish slang for 'Wow!' or 'Hey!'

THE WITNESS SETS THE SCENE

We were exhausted. We had landed on December 2, at a place known as Las Coloradas beach. We had lost almost all our equipment and trudged endlessly through saltwater swamps. Almost the entire troop was suffering open blisters on their feet; but boots and fungal infections were not our only enemies. We reached Cuba following a seven-day voyage across the Gulf of Mexico and the Caribbean Sea, without food, in a poorly maintained boat, almost everyone plagued by seasickness from not being used to sea travel. We left the port of Tuxpan on November 25, a day with a stiff wind when all sea travel was prohibited. All this had left its mark on our troop made up of raw recruits who had never seen combat.

All we had left of our equipment for war was our rifles, cartridge belts, and a few wet rounds of ammunition. Our medical supplies had vanished, and most of our backpacks had been left behind in the swamps. The previous night we had passed through a cane field. We had managed to satisfy our hunger and thirst by eating sugarcane, but lacking experience we had left a trail of cane peelings. Not that the guards following our steps needed any trail, for it had been our guide - we found out years later - who betrayed us and brought them to us. When we stopped to rest the night before, we let him go - an error we were to repeat several times during our long struggle.

Character Profiles

Fidel Castro

Fidel Castro was born in August 1926 in Cuba, to wealthy Spanish immigrants who owned a sugar cane plantation. Fidel graduated from Havana University with a law degree in 1945. He was a bright student, with the unusual ability to memorize entire books. When Fidel Castro met Che Guevara in 1954, Castro was a political exile in Mexico following his attack on the Moncada army barracks in Santiage de Cuba. The two quickly became revolutionary soul mates, committed to helping Latin Americans throw off the vestiges of colonialism and narrow the divide between rich and poor.

Ernesto 'Che' Guevara

Ernesto Guevara de la Serna was born in June 1928 in Argentina into an upper middle-class family. At the age of two, Ernesto developed the severe asthmatic condition he refers to in his account, and the family moved to the drier climate of Alta Gracia, Cordoba, where they thought Ernesto would be better off. Most of his education was conducted at home. He read widely from his father's library, covering the works of Marx and Freud whilst still in his early teens. In 1948, Ernesto enrolled at the University of Buenos Aires to study medicine. He qualified as a doctor in 1953 (his medical condition meant he escaped military service) and it was about this time that he began to be politically active. He met Fidel Castro in 1954, through a Peruvian Marxist, Hilda Gadea, who he later married, and became involved with the planning of a Cuban revolution.

THE WITNESS'S ACCOUNT

On the verge of collapse, we would walk a short distance and then beg for a long rest. At noon we noticed unusual activity. Planes began to circle. Some of our group continued cutting and eating sugarcane, not realizing they were visible to those flying the enemy planes, circling at slow speed and low altitude. *Compañero*[1] Montané and I were leaning against a tree talking about our respective children, eating our rations - half a sausage and two crackers - when we heard a shot. Within seconds, a hail of bullets - at least that's how it seemed to us - descended on our group of eighty-two men. My rifle was not one of the best; I had deliberately asked for it because I was in terrible physical condition due to a prolonged asthma attack I had endured throughout our voyage, and I did not want to waste a good weapon.

I can hardly remember what followed. After the initial burst of gunfire, Almeida approached requesting orders, but there was no one to issue

1 – Comrade.

them. Fidel had tried in vain to gather everybody. The surprise had been too great and the gunfire too heavy. Almeida ran back to take charge of his group. A *compañero* dropped a box of ammunition at my feet. I pointed to it, and he answered me with an anguished expression which seemed to say, 'It's too late for ammunition.' (He was later murdered by Batista's henchmen.)

I was faced with the dilemma of choosing between my devotion to medicine and my duty as a revolutionary soldier. There, at my feet, was a backpack full of medicine and a box of ammunition. They were too heavy to carry both. I picked up the ammunition. I remember Faustino Pérez, on his knees in the bushes, firing his submachine gun. Near me, a *compañero* named Albentosa was walking toward the cane field. A burst of gunfire hit us both.

"He showed me a bullet wound that appeared to have pierced his lungs"

I felt a sharp blow to my chest and a wound in my neck; I thought for certain I was dead. Albentosa, vomiting blood and bleeding profusely from a deep wound made by a .45-calibre bullet, screamed something like, 'They've killed me.' Flat on the ground, I said to Faustino, 'I'm fucked,' and Faustino, still shooting, looked at me and told me it was nothing, but I saw in his eyes he considered me as good as dead. I began to think about the best way to die, since all seemed lost. I remembered an old Jack London story in which the hero, aware that he is about to freeze to death in the Alaskan ice, leans against a tree and prepares to die with dignity. Someone shouted that we should surrender, and I heard [another] voice shouting, 'No one surrenders here!'

[José] Ponce approached me, agitated and breathing hard. He showed me a bullet wound that appeared to have pierced his lungs. He told me he was wounded and I replied, indifferently, that I was as well. Then Ponce, along with other unhurt *compañeros*, crawled toward the cane field. For a moment I was alone, just waiting to die. Almeida urged me to go on, and despite the intense pain I dragged myself into the cane field. Then everything blurred - low-flying airplanes strafing the field, adding to the confusion - amid scenes that were at once Dantesque and grotesque, such as an overweight combatant trying to hide behind a single sugarcane stalk, or a man who kept yelling for silence in the din of gunfire.

With Almeida leading, we reached the safety of the woods. shouts of 'Fire!' were heard from the cane field and columns of flame began to rise. But I was thinking more of the bitterness of defeat and the imminence of my death. We walked until darkness made it impossible to go on, and decided to sleep huddled together in a heap. We were starving and thirsty, the mosquitoes adding to our misery.

This was our baptism of fire, December 5, 1956, on the outskirts of Niquero. Such was the beginning of forging what would become the Rebel Army.

Batista and the Cuban Revolution

For over 25 years one man dominated Cuban politics. That man was Rubén Fulgencio Batista Zaldivar. He was born in 1901 to working class Cuban parents who had both fought for Cuban indpendence from Spain. As a young man he worked in a variety of different, low paid jobs, before joining the army as a sergeant. He came to power in Cuba twice, the first time was in 1933, when he organized the Sergeants' Revolt, and siezed power from the dictatorial regime of Gerado Machado y Morales to become army chief of staff. His first term in government is generally described by historians as successful. Batista was a very good judge of men, and managed to secure the backing of the civil service, the army and organized labour. His opponents were either gunned down in the street by government agents, or they just disappeared into thin air. Batista made himself a huge amount of money, but also ran the government successfully, expanding the educational system, sponsoring a huge number of public works and fostering the growth of the economy. It was also during this time that Batista met, and formed a friendship with, gangster Meyer Lansky, and Mafia relations with Cuba improved significantly.

When his first term ended, in 1944, he travelled abroad and settled for a while in Florida, where he 'invested' some of the huge sums he had acquired in Cuba. While living sumptuously in Daytona Beach, Florida in 1948, Batista was elected to the Cuban senate. Four years later he ran once more for President, but the polls showed him in last place. He was not expected to win democratically, so, three months before the elections were due to close, he staged a coup. Batista took power with help from a nationalist section of the army, and suspended aspects of the Cuban constitution, including the right for workers to strike. He also began paving the way for large scale gambling in Havana. Meanwhile a young lawyer named Fidel Castro, was already planning a rebellion.

THE ASSASSINATION OF PRESIDENT KENNEDY

He started to bring his head up to look at me and just as he did the shot rang out

WITNESSED BY
PHILIP BEN HATHAWAY
AND JEAN L. HILL

On 22 November 1963, President John F. Kennedy was shot during a motorcade through the streets of Dallas, Texas. In the aftermath of the assassination, the Warren Commission (which decided that the assassin acted alone) looked at formal affidavit evidence from as many as 74 witnesses to this historic event – yet in spite of this thorough trawling for the truth, the witnesses did not agree about what happened. Here are two witnesses supporting the idea that Lee Harvey Oswald was *not* a lone assassin.

THE WITNESSES

1) Philip Ben Hathaway was a 28 year-old who worked in the Research and Development Department of the Lone Star Gas Company. He gave his statement to the Dallas Police Dept on the day of the shooting.

2) Mrs Jean L. Hill was a Dallas schoolteacher. She was standing on the south side of Elm Street in Dealey Plaza, directly opposite the grassy knoll.

Jean Hill is known as The Woman in Red, because of the long red raincoat she was wearing on the day of the assassination. At the moment when Kennedy was shot in the head, Jean Hill was only slightly behind Kennedy and 21 feet away from him. This makes her the closest witness (outside the car) to the assassination.

THE WITNESS'S ACCOUNT

1) Philip Ben Hathaway

Just before noon today, my friend John Lawrence, who works with me, and I and two other friends left the Texaco Building where we work going to the parade. While we were walking up Akard towards Main Street we passed a man who was carrying a rifle in a gun case. I saw this man walking towards me, walking towards Commerce, and took particular attention to him because of his size. I am 6 foot 5 inches and weigh 200 pounds. This man was very tall, approx 6 foot 6 inches or 6 foot 7 inches over 250 pounds, very thick and big through the chest, in his thirties, dirty blonde [ie light brown] hair worn in a crew cut. Was wearing a grey colored business suit with white dress shirt, fair complexion.

I remarked to my friend that there was a guy carrying a gun in all this crowd and made the remark that he was probably a secret service man. I could very easily identify this man if I ever saw him again. The gun case was holding a rifle: I could tell there was a gun in it as without a gun, it would have been limp, but it was heavy and he was carrying it by the handle and the barrel of the gun was up at a 45 degree angle.

We can place the time that we saw this man walking with the gun as I recall someone in the crowd asking for the time and they said it was 11.50 am.

Character Profiles

. . . .

John F Kennedy

John Fitzgerald Kennedy was born in Brookline, Massachusetts in 1917, to Joseph P Kennedy and Rose Fitzgerald, an Irish Roman Catholic family. The Fitzgerald and the Kennedy families were both heavily involved in local politics. Both his grandfathers were important political figures in Boston and his father served as American ambassador to Great Britain. In 1940, Kennedy graduated from Harvard with a science degree. In 1941 he joined the US Navy as an intelligence officer, but when America joined World War II, he transferred to a motor torpedo boat squadron and was given command of a PT boat. In 1943, in the South Pacific, his boat was hit by a Japanese destroyer. Kennedy sustained the back injury that gave him serious pain for the rest of his life. Back in the United States he continued to serve in the

Navy, and worked as a journalist before being elected to the House of Representatives as a Democrat in 1946. Over the next couple of years he established himself as a staunch supporter of President Harry S. Truman. He favoured progressive taxation, the development of low cost public housing, the extension of social welfare and the relaxation of immigration laws. Kennedy believed in the black civil rights campaign and wanted to see the power of the Mafia over the unions reduced.

....

Lee Harvey Oswald

Lee Harvey Oswald was certainly a confused individual, but debate continues as to whether he was the lone assassin. Oswald was born in New Orleans in 1939, to Robert Oswald and his wife Marguerite. His father died two months before Lee Harvey was born, and when he was only three years old, Marguerite, who was struggling to cope on her own, sent him to live at the Bethlehem Children's home. He eventually returned to live with his mother when she remarried a man named Edwin Ekdahl. The marriage didn't last and Marguerite moved her three young sons once again, this time to Fort Worth and later again to New York. Oswald was considered fairly bright by his teachers, but the constant moving meant his behaviour deteriorated and he was sent away yet again, this time to a detention centre where he received psychiatric treatment. Oswald became involved in radical politics in 1956, when he began reading Marxist literature and joined the Young People's Socialist League. In fact, Oswald seems to have been a serial 'joiner'. He either joined, or tried to join, the US Marines, The Soviet Union, The Fair Play for Cuba Committee and the American Communist Party. Perhaps this was his way of dealing with a lonely childhood spent moving from one place to another.

Involvement in radical political groups may have given him a feeling of belonging. Until the fateful moment when he killed Kennedy, Oswald had achieved nothing at all. It was as if that was the only thing he could do to make people remember him, that was his only way into history.

THE WITNESS'S ACCOUNT

2) Jean Hill

Jean Hill was interviewed by Arlen Specter for the Warren Commission on 24 March 1964.

Specter: She [Mary Moorman] had a camera with her?

Jean Hill: Yes; a Polaroid. We had been taking pictures all morning.

Specter: And tell me what you observed as the President's motorcade passed by.

Jean Hill: He [Kennedy] drew even with us. We were standing on the kerb and I jumped to the edge and yelled, 'Hey, we want to take your picture,' to him and he was looking down in the seat - he and Mrs. Kennedy and their heads were turned toward the middle of the car looking down at something in the seat, and I was so afraid he was going to look the other way because there were a lot of people across the street and we were the only people down there in that area, and just as I yelled, 'Hey,' to him, he started to bring his head up to look at me and just as he did the shot rang out. Mary took the picture and fell on the ground and of course there were more shots.

Specter: How many shots were there altogether?

Jean Hill: I have always said there were some four to six shots. There were three shots - one right after the other, and a distinct pause, and then I heard more.

Specter: How long a time elapsed from the first

to the third of what you described as the first three shots?

Jean Hill: They were rapidly fired.

Specter: Could you give me an estimate on the time span on those three shots?

Jean Hill: No; I don't think I can.

Specter: Now, how many shots followed what you described as the first three shots?

Jean Hill: I think there were at least four or five shots and perhaps six, but I know there were more than three.

The Cuban Missile Crisis

The Cuban missile crisis is generally remembered as the closest the world has ever come to all-out nuclear war. During this 14 day period in October 1962, the United States was on the highest level of alert ever, and Soviet forces in Cuba were fully prepared to defend the island using whatever means necessary. The crisis began when the Soviets, who were falling dangerously behind in the arms race, decided to install intermediate range nuclear missiles on Cuban soil so they would be in a position to strike the US if they needed to. The US had missiles installed in Turkey, and were already able to target Russia if they wanted to, but the Russians were not in a position to strike back, that is until Cuba agreed to allow the Soviets to use the island for military purposes in return for protection against a possible US invasion. On 15 October 1962, reconnaissance photos revealed that Soviet missiles were under construction in Cuba and the US government, went into a state of panic. President Kennedy immediately gathered 12 of his most highly respected advisors to help him handle the crisis. After seven days of intense talks Kennedy decided to impose a naval quarantine around Cuba in order to prevent any more weapons arriving there from the USSR, but that didn't solve the existing problem. On 22 October Kennedy announced the discovery of the missiles, and the US counter measures to the American public, he also proclaimed that any missile launched from Cuba would be regarded as an attack on the United States. The president, supported by his brother Robert, stood firm. On 28 October 1962 tensions finally eased when the Soviet leader, Khrushchev, agreed to dismantle the missiles in Cuba and return them to Russia in return for an assurance from the United States that they would not invade Cuba.

THE WITNESS'S ACCOUNT

3) Jean Hill gave the following version in a talk in November 1991.

I knew the President was never going to look at me, so I yelled, 'Hey Mr. President, I want to take your picture!' Just then his hands came up and the shots started ringing out. I looked across the street and I saw them shooting from the knoll. I did get the impression that day that there was more than one shooter. Mary was on the grass shouting, 'Get down! They're shooting!' I looked up and saw this man, moving rather quickly in front of the School Book Depository toward the railroad tracks, heading west, toward the area where I had seen the man shooting on the knoll. So, I thought to myself, 'This man is getting away. I've got to do something. I've got to catch him.' I jumped out into the street.

I ran across and went up the hill. When I got there a hand came down on my shoulder, and it was a firm grip. This man said, 'You're coming with me.' And I said, 'No, I can't come with you, I have to get this man.' I'm not very good at doing what I'm told. He showed me ID. It said Secret Service. It looked official to me. I tried to turn away from him and he said a second time, 'You're going with me.' At this point, a second man came and grabbed me from the other side.

They took me to the Records Building, to a room on the fourth floor. There were two guys sitting there at a window that overlooked 'the killing zone', where you could see all of the goings on. You got the impression that they had been sitting there for a long time. They asked me what I had seen, and it became clear that they knew what I had seen. They asked me how many shots I had heard and I told them four to six. And they said, 'No, you didn't. There were three shots.' I said, 'Well, I know what I heard,' and they told me, 'You would be very wise to keep your mouth shut.'

A UFO SEEN FROM APOLLO 11

There was something out there… close enough to be observed – and what could it be?

WITNESSED BY
BUZZ ALDRIN

It was three days and 200,000 miles into the Apollo 11 flight to the Moon that the incident occurred. A mysterious object appeared, travelling alongside Apollo 11. The crew wondered if it might be the S-IVB, the final stage of the rocket, which had been jettisoned two days earlier. To check whether it was indeed the S-IVB, the crew asked Mission Control for its current location. A cryptic enquiry was sent from Apollo 11, the significance of which was lost on Mission Control.

Apollo 11: Do you have any idea where the S-IVB is with respect to us?

Mission Control: Stand by... Apollo 11, Houston. The S-IVB is about 6,000 nautical miles from you now. Over.

THE WITNESS

Colonel Edwin E. Aldrin is better known as Buzz Aldrin. He was one of the three-man crew of the Apollo 11 mission, together with Michael Collins and Neil Armstrong.

THE WITNESS'S ACCOUNT

1) In a television documentary interview

There was something out there that, uh, was close enough to be observed – and what could it be? Mike [Collins] decided he thought he could see it in the telescope and he was able to do that and when it was in one position it had a series of ellipses, but when you made it real sharp it was sort of L-shaped. That didn't tell us very much. Now, obviously, the three of us were not going to blurt out, 'Hey, Houston, we got something moving alongside of us and we don't know what it is, you know, can you tell us what it is?' We weren't about to do that, 'cause we know that those transmissions would be heard by all sorts of people and who knows what somebody would have demanded that we turn back because of Aliens or whatever the reason. So we didn't do that, but we did decide we'd just cautiously ask Houston where, how far away, was the S-IVB? And a few moments later, why, they came back and said something like it was 6,000 miles away because of the manoeuvre, so we really didn't think we were looking at something that far away. So we decided that, after a while of watching it, it was time to go to sleep and not to talk about it any more until we came back and [went through] debriefing.

The Apollo Program

The mission statement for NASA's Apollo program must have seemed, to most Americans, inplausible in the extreme when it was first announced in 1961. The idea of landing a man on the moon and bringing him safely back to earth again was well beyond the reach of most people's imaginations. However, there was more to the Apollo program's goal than landing a man on the moon simply for the sake of it. NASA intended to establish technology to meet other national interests in space, to achieve pre-eminence in space for the United States, to carry out a program of scientific exploration of the moon and to develop a capacity to work in a lunar environment. Between 1969 and 1972, six of the Apollo missions, numbers 11, 12, 14, 15, 16 and 17, achieved these goals. Apollos 7 and 9 were never intended to land on the moon, but were Earth orbiting missions set to test the command and lunar modules. Apollos 8 and 10 orbited the moon, and returned photographs of the lunar surface in preparation for the big one: Apollo 11. It was John F Kennedy who, in 1961, announced that the United States intended to become the first country to fund and execute a lunar space mission. Kennedy was assassinated before the US succeeded, but it was his administration that set the ball rolling. All the Apollo spacecraft were built to the same three-part design. The command module comprised the crew's quarters and the flight control section. The service module provided the propulsion and the spacecraft support system. The lunar module could detach from the other two parts and enable two members of the crew to land on the surface of the moon.

Character Profile

Buzz Aldrin

Edwin Eugene Aldrin Jr was born in 1930 in New Jersey. As a young man, Buzz (his sister's nickname for him) was educated at West Point military academy. After coming third in his class with a Science degree, he joined the US Air Force as a jet pilot and saw action during the Korean War. He flew in over 60 combat missions in F86 Sabres. When the Korean war came to an end, Buzz attended the prestigious Massachusetts Institute of Technology (MIT) where he studied for a degree in aeronautics. In 1963, he was selected by NASA to take part in the space program as one of the third group of astronauts. Following the tragic deaths of Elliot See and Charles Bassett of the Gemini 9 prime crew, Aldrin was promoted to back up crew for the repeat mission, Gemini 9A. It was during this mission that Aldrin proved himself as a resourceful and cool-headed team member, and earned his place as a pilot on the Gemini 12 mission. Finally, on 20 July 1969, Buzz Aldrin achieved a life long ambition to land on the moon alongside his friend and colleague Neil Armstrong, as part of the Apollo 11 moon landing.

....

Michael Collins

Major General Michael Collins was selected by NASA alongside Buzz Aldrin as part of the third group of astronauts. Having passed basic training, each astronaut was given a specialization. Collins was given his first choice of pressure suits and EVAs – extra vehicular activity, or spacewalking. His first journey into space was as part of the Gemini 10 mission, during which he successfully operated two rendezvous with other spacecraft, performed two EVAs and took part in 15 experiments. His second, and last, journey into space was as part of the Apollo 11 crew, accompanied by Buzz Aldrin and Neil Armstrong. Collins had the job of orbiting the moon in the command module while Aldrin and Armstrong completed their moon landing and moonwalk.

....

Neil Armstrong

Neil Armstrong is the most famous member of the Apollo 11 team because, on 20 July 1969, he became the first person to walk on the surface of the moon. He was born in 1930 and was fascinated with aviation from an early age. He began studying for a degree in aeronautical engineering at Purdue University, but in 1949, at the beginning of the Korean War, the US Navy called him into active service as a pilot. While stationed in Korea, he flew a total of 78 combat missions in Navy Panther jets. In 1952 he returned to Purdue University to complete his bachelor degree in aeronautics, graduating in 1955. From university Armstrong joined NASA and became a civilian test pilot assigned to test the X-15 rocket airplane, before joining the space program in 1962. He made his first journey into space as part of the crew of Gemini 8, alongside David R Scott. The two men performed a successful docking operation between Gemini 8 and another uninhabited spacecraft – the Agena rocket.

THE WITNESS'S ACCOUNT

2) **The Apollo 11 technical debriefing.**

Aldrin: The first unusual thing we saw I guess was one day out or something pretty close to the

Moon. It had a sizeable dimension to it, so we put the monocular on it.

Collins: How did we see this thing? Did we just look out the window and there it was?

Aldrin: Yes, and we weren't sure but what it might be the S-IVB. We called the ground and were told the S-IVB was 6,000 miles away. We had a problem with the high gain about this time, didn't we?

Collins: There was something. We felt a bump or maybe I just imagined it.

Armstrong: He was wondering whether the MESA had come off.

Collins: I don't guess we felt anything.

Aldrin: Of course, we were seeing all sorts of little objects going by as the various dumps and then we happened to see this one brighter object going by. We couldn't think of anything else it could be other than the S-IVB. We looked at it through the monocular and it seemed to have a bit of an L shape to it.

Armstrong: Like an open suitcase.

Aldrin: We were in PTC at the time so each of us had a chance to take a look at this and it certainly seemed to be within our vicinity and of a very sizeable dimension.

Armstrong: We should say it was right at the limit of the resolution of the eye [ie a very long way away]. It was very difficult to tell what shape it was.

Aldrin: So then I got down in the LEB and started looking for it in the optics. We were grossly misled because with the sextant off focus what we saw appeared to be a cylinder.

Armstrong: Or really two rings.

Aldrin: Yes.

Armstrong: Two rings. Two connected rings.

Aldrin: Yes.

Collins: No, it looked like a hollow cylinder to me. It didn't look like two connected rings. You could see this thing tumbling and, when it came around end-on, you could look right down its guts. It was a hollow cylinder. But then you could change the focus on the sextant and it would be replaced by this open book shape. It was really weird.

Aldrin: I guess there's not too much more to say about it other than it wasn't a cylinder.

Collins: It was during this period when we thought it was a cylinder that we inquired about the S-IVB and we'd almost convinced ourselves that's what it had to be. But we don't have any more conclusions than that really. The fact that we didn't see it much past this one period – we don't really have a conclusion as to what it might have been, how big it was, or how far away it was. It was something that wasn't part of the urine dump, we're pretty sure of that.

....

"whatever it was, it was only a hundred miles or so away"

....

THE WITNESS'S ACCOUNT

3) In *Return to Earth* by Buzz Aldrin

In the middle of one evening, Houston time, I found myself idly staring out the window of the *Columbia* and saw something that looked a bit unusual. It appeared brighter than any star and not quite the pinpoints of light that stars are. I pointed this out to Mike and Neil, and the three of us were beset with curiosity. With the help of the monocular we guessed that whatever it was, it was only a hundred miles or so away. Looking through our sextant we found it occasionally formed a cylinder, but when the sextant's focus was adjusted it had a sort of illuminated 'L' look to it. It had a shape of some sort – we all agreed on that – but exactly what it was we couldn't pin down. We asked Houston some casual questions: 'How far away is the Saturn third stage?' The response was in the vicinity of 6,000 miles. That wasn't it.

It could possibly have been one of the panels of the Saturn third stage which fly off to expose the LM and cannot be traced from Earth. We could see it for about forty-five seconds at a time as the ship rotated, and we watched it on and off for about an hour. We debated whether or not to tell the ground we had spotted something, and decided against it. Our reason was simple: the UFO people would descend on the message in hordes, setting off another rash of UFO spottings on Earth. We concluded it was most likely one of the panels. Its course in no way conflicted with ours, and it presented no danger. We dropped the matter there.

Despite having a clear view of the UFO, the Apollo 11 crew were wary of reporting it to Mission Control.

The crews of several space flights saw them. The UFO sighting from Apollo 11 was never satisfactorily explained, and never officially acknowledged. People working on the project later spoke of their conviction that UFOs existed. This led to concern at NASA, who pressed crew members not to talk in public about the matter.

MEETING POPE JOHN PAUL II

There was a palpable presence that surrounded him, an almost electric power

WITNESSED BY
THOM HARTMANN

An evening audience with Pope John Paul II in August 1998 at Castel Gandolfo, the Pope's summer residence. The high levels of security and the Pope's poor physical state were both legacies of the assassination attempt in St Peter's Square seventeen years earlier, on 13 May 1981. The Pope was hit by three bullets and was lucky to survive.

THE WITNESS

Thom Hartmann is an American writer on democracy and spirituality. He was invited to an audience as the author of a book called *The Prophet's Way*. His description of a papal audience mixes the objective and factual with the intensely subjective. Did John Paul really have an aura?

THE WITNESS'S ACCOUNT

Louise and I walked through the tourist shops, stopped in an open-air café for a glass of beer, and found a shop that sold Catholic and papal souvenirs, where we were able to purchase a refrigerator magnet with the Pope's picture on it. Swiss Guards, wearing bright orange and blue pantaloons designed by Michelangelo, stood before the ancient, thirty-foot-high brass-covered door to the castle, their lances at arms, and several men with ear-pieces and sharp looks - the Papal equivalent of the Secret Service - milled around the area, their black suits buttoned to conceal the guns they wore in their shoulder holsters. At seven o'clock, the doors to the castle were opened. We presented our invitations, were scanned with hand-held metal detectors and allowed into the courtyard of Castel Gandolfo.

The Hungarian National Orchestra had set up their music stands in the center of the courtyard. Chairs were placed to the left and right of the orchestra, and Louise and I were directed to chairs with our names on them. Above us in the open-air courtyard was stretched from all four walls a huge canvas sheet, protecting us from the

419

sun. About 30 feet away, was an alcove in the wall with a 15-foot-high bronze statue of Saint Peter. In front of the statue were seven chairs and a gold-covered throne. About 200 people altogether came into the seats on either side of the orchestra. Dr Juhar, the organizer of the event, came over and gave all of us in the front row clip-on hand-written badges to wear. 'This means you are to personally meet with His Holiness,' she said.

At 7.30, the huge doors into the castle were closed and locked with a loud thud, shutting out the sounds of the tourists in the street: the Swiss Guard took up their traditional positions, lances crossed. The room became silent.

At some unheard cue, everybody in the room stood. We heard a shuffling gait, step-clump, step-clump, and the Pope shuffled slowly in. The courtyard was so silent I could hear the laboured breathing. He had a pronounced dowager's hump, and he was walking with some pain. His skin looked fresh-scrubbed pink, and his forehead was wrinkled as if he were concentrating. Nonetheless, there was a palpable presence that surrounded him, an almost electric power. At this moment the sun was setting and the air in the courtyard changed; it seemed as if it had thickened, the sunlight brightened, the yellow walls darkened.

The Cardinal and a Priest held each of his elbows, steering him to his throne. Before he sat, he looked around the room and waved at us in a gesture that went from shoulder to waist, up and down, hand outstretched, with his right hand: a Papal blessing. Then, when he was seated, a priest reached over and arranged his clothes and his sash.

My first sensation of him was that he was very, very old and frail. Yet there is the power to say words which could change the world. The Pope leads over a billion Catholics. There followed a period of about three minutes of silence. Most of the visitors were watching the Pope, whose head was tilted slightly to his left and down, his eyes thin slits as he looked around the room. I noticed the pace of his breathing and matched it, trying to get as close to synchrony with him as I could, and saw a flicker of his eyes in my direction. I continued to match his breathing and to imitate his posture. There was an aura about him. I don't know if it was a trick of my eyes or what, but it seemed that there was something radiating from him. After a minute or two, I crossed my hands in my lap: he followed, which startled me. I sat that way for a minute longer, still following each of his in and out breaths with mine, and then separated my hands. At that moment, he moved his hands to the arms of his throne and nodded, as if he'd made a decision.

Dr Juhar walked to a microphone and made a brief speech, mentioning the need to bring Catholics and non-Catholics together, and the value of music in doing this. The Pope smiled and nodded to the conductor. The music which lasted for about fifty minutes was beautiful. They played Mendelssohn's *Violin Concerto*. I looked at the program to see who the performers were, and was stunned to see four names at the bottom of the program listed as 'honoured guests' (in Italian). One was Gottfried Müller, the other 'Dr Thomas Hartmann', and the other two heads of European parliaments seated with us. After the music, the Pope thanked the musicians. He spoke briefly in Hungarian to the orchestra, eliciting huge smiles.

Those of us with the badges formed a line. Most were dignitaries from Germany. I'd been sitting next to the head of the German Bundestag. Louise stood in front of me in line, shook [the Pope's] hand, and had a brief conversation with him. I was next and, with the official Vatican photographers clicking away, he shook my hand firmly (the pictures will arrive in the mail in a week or two). I asked him a very personal (for me) question, and he gave me an interesting answer. As I turned from shaking his hand, the priest who'd been sitting behind the Pope handed me a Rosary that had been blessed by the pontiff:

Louise had been given one, too. And then I walked back to the front-row seats.

The Pope again gave his blessing to the audience, bringing applause, and then was assisted back into the castle by the Cardinal and a priest.

THE 9/11 TERRORIST ATTACKS

Looking out the window I saw this rain of fire coming down and it blew out the windows on the 44th floor

WITNESSED BY
MATTHEW CORNELOUS
AND DAVID LIM

On 11 September 2001 a group of Al Qaeda
terrorists hi-jacked three US passenger planes
and deliberately crashed them into the Pentagon
in Washington and the twin towers of the World
Trade Center in New York. The towers collapsed
and altogether 2,752 innocent people were
killed.

THE WITNESSES

1) Matthew Cornelous was working for the Port
Authority aviation department in the World
Trade Center. He was interviewed by the press.

2) David Lim was a Port Authority police officer
who was working in Tower Two with a bomb-
sniffing dog called Sirius. He gave evidence to the
9/11 Commission.

THE WITNESSES' ACCOUNTS

1) Matthew Cornelous

Sixty-fifth floor, that's where I work. I arrived at work a little bit early today. I was just putting my stuff away and all of a sudden we heard a loud crash. The building started shaking, kind of moving like a wave. I had no idea. We figured an airplane had hit it. Everybody started screaming, 'Move away from the windows! Let's get out of here!' And we saw debris fall past the window on the north side.

We really had no idea at all what had happened until we exited the building. We took the stairs. We made it pretty fast down to the fortieth floor. And from there, the smoke got a little bit thick and it was a lot slower. We made it about a floor every two minutes. It was packed, it was a virtual traffic jam in the staircase. Up and down. It was very full.

Everybody maintained calm really well: I was impressed with that. I think for some people it brought back memories of the bombing [in 1993], people who'd been there before when that happened. But I was amazed, really. We got into the stairway, we were moving down. The fire department, when we were coming out, said, 'Move to the left, move to the left. Everyone complied.

A couple of people started crying. It wasn't quiet, people were talking - in fact someone was laughing: I thought that was strange. But we didn't understand the full severity of the situation. Once we got down, they put us on the plaza level, which was disturbing. There was a lot of debris in the plaza level, a lot of carnage.

We moved out the back toward Broadway. The police were saying, 'Don't look back.' We made it about half a block and I saw the other tower on fire and I couldn't believe it. . . We never had any fear of the building collapse.

2) David Lim

I was working with my partner, Sirius. I had just finished up searching trucks with my partner and I had retired to my office to do my paperwork and have a little breakfast.

8.45 am all that changed. I was in the basement of Tower Two, yet I felt the shock of the first plane hitting Tower 1. I secured my partner in his kennel, told him that I had to go help the people - and I figured he'd be safe there while I went to assist. Unfortunately, that was the last time I saw him.

I was assisting people out of the A staircase as they were coming out of the building. Somebody screamed that a body was outside on the plaza. I went over to investigate. Just as I did that, another body fell about ten feet away.

I headed up into the building to assist. I kept on going up, telling people to keep going down: down is good. I remember running into people that were burned, asking for help. What I did was I assigned those people to people that were healthy to help get them down. I felt the greater good was for me to get to a higher point to try to assist those people upstairs.

And sure enough, just as I was starting to get the people down, I felt another collision on the left side. Looking out the window I saw this rain of fire coming down and it blew out the windows on the 44th floor. Fortunately, I was not burned, but I was knocked to the ground by the concussion. The building now was starting to shake. As we were going down, I was clearing the floors, getting people that were left behind. Most of them were either handicapped or elderly, but we had to go.

We got to about the 35th floor, in that general area. I don't remember specifically when I felt the building shaking. I thought for sure that my building was collapsing. Then I heard on the radio something I will never forget, 'Tower 2 is down, all units evacuate Tower 1.'

As we were going down, and now we were starting to lose power in the building, the lights were going on and off.

I got down to the fifth floor and that is where I met Josephine Harris and Ladder Company 6. Josephine Harris, who is a Port Authority employee, had walked down 72 flights, and she had a bad leg problem and she could go no further. I grabbed Josephine by one arm, Firefighter Tommy Falco grabbed the other arm, with Billy Butler right behind us; we started going down.

Well, one more flight down was as far as we got and the building started coming down. I knew that was it because the other building was already gone. I knew it was coming down. All I could think of is, well, protect Josephine from the debris. So me and Tommy were covering her and it started coming. You could feel the wind of pushing down as they were compressing through the building, you could hear the sound. It was like an onrushing locomotive or an avalanche. You could almost feel the sound of the floors pancaking on top of each other as they were collapsing. As we all know, they collapsed straight down. And they just kept coming and coming. I guess my final thoughts were about my family.

When the debris stopped falling first I thought I had died. But then I heard a voice. We couldn't see each other. It was totally black. We couldn't breathe. We had to try to breathe through our shirts, but we were in fairly good shape. We were alive. We saw a light over the sixth-floor staircase and our first thought was that the floor had power in it and it was virtually, or at least partially, intact, we could make our stand there.

As that light got brighter, it turned out to be the sun. We were standing on top of what was left of the World Trade Center. By all the engineers and everybody else that tried to figure this out, there's no reason why I should be sitting here talking to you right now. It was just a small sliver of staircase from the sixth floor down to the first floor, that preserved our lives.

I grieve for all those that I knew that day, I grieve for those that I will never know, but I also grieve for the best partner I ever had.

INDEX

AUTHOR BIOGRAPHY

Rodney Castleden has a passionate interest in history and archaeology, and has written extensively on these subjects over the last thirty years. Reviewers and readers have commended his meticulous research, fluency of expression and the originality of his ideas. He is the author of more than thirty books, including *People Who Changed the World*, *Natural Disasters That Changed the World*, *The Making of Stonehenge*, *King Arthur*, *Minoans*, *Mycenaeans* and *The Attack on Troy*. Rodney lives on Blatchington Hill in Seaford, East Sussex.

ACKNOWLEDGMENTS

Every effort has been made to contact the holders of the copyright material. However, the publishers will be glad to rectify in future editions any inadvertent omissions brought to their attention.

The publisher would like to thank the following for permission to reproduce copyright material:

Meeting Elizabeth I, by Andre Hurault Sieur de Maisse, translated by G.B.Harrison and R.A Jones in 1931, copyright: Duckworth Press.

Sir Thomas More, by Erasmus, as published in 'They Saw It Happen', edited by C. Routh, copyright: Blackwell Press.

The discovery of Tutankhamun's tomb, by Howard Carter, copyright: Griffith Institute, University of Oxford.

The Bombing of Guernica, by Noel Monks, copyright: Noel Monks. This account appears courtesy of the Monks family, permission granted by John Monks.

Meeting Pope John Paul II, by Thom Hartmann, copyright: Thom Hartmann.

PICTURE CREDITS